"Breaking Through "Bitch" shows women that the skills that they have learned based on expectations for being female in society—listening, collaboration, and thinking outside the box, for example—are actually very valuable skills for business leaders to have. For women who wish to get to the top of corporate America as it stands today, it is important to understand how to leverage these skills to achieve your goals. This book provides great insights about how successful business women are doing this today and how future female business leaders can model these behaviors at work."

—Katina Sawyer, PhD, assistant professor of psychology, graduate programs in Human Resource Development, Villanova University

"Breaking Through "Bitch" is much more than a provocative title—it's a book that uses data and research to identify the competencies necessary for women to succeed by leading collaboratively—without being called the 'b' word. Dr. Mitchell has made the case that it is a mistake to undervalue women's natural abilities and strengths, for collaborative leadership is taking the day now and in the future. I'm sharing this book with other leaders in my network—male and female—and I'm encouraging my college-aged son and his friends to read it as well."

—Carol Pandza, senior leader, Human Resources, Philadelphia, Pa.

"Mitchell's Women's Leadership Blueprint is truly 'fit for purpose' not just for would be women executives but for aspiring men as well."

—J. Glade Holman, partner, Park Li Group

"Carol Mitchell shows us how to embrace who we are and how we lead to be effective in the workplace and beyond. Whether you are a young professional just starting on your journey or a seasoned professional looking for reassurance and a few tweaks to improve your effectiveness, there's something here for you."

—Mary Pat Knauss, President, Board of Directors of Wings for Success

"This book is a 'must read' for every woman manager who wants to improve her leadership skills. Carol Mitchell confronts directly a lot of concerns and questions that most woman managers are thinking and feeling."

—Steve Heinen, PhD, President, Steve Heinen & Associates

BREAKING THROUGH "BITCH"

HOW WOMEN CAN SHATTER STEREOTYPES AND LEAD FEARLESSLY

Carol Vallone Mitchell

FOREWORD BY ANNIE MCKEE
best-selling coauthor of *Primal Leadership*

The Career Press, Inc.
Wayne, NJ

BREAKING THROUGH "BITCH"
EDITED BY JODI BRANDON
TYPESET BY KRISTIN GOBLE
Cover design by Howard Grossman
Printed in the U.S.A.

To order this title, please call toll-free 1-800-CAREER-1 (NJ and Canada: 201-848-0310) to order using VISA or MasterCard, or for further information on books from Career Press.

The Career Press, Inc.
12 Parish Drive
Wayne, NJ 07470
www.careerpress.com

Library of Congress Cataloging-in-Publication Data

Mitchell, Carol Vallone, author.
  Breaking through "bitch" : how women can shatter stereotypes and lead fearlessly / by Carol Vallone Mitchell ; foreword by Annie McKee.
       pages cm
  Includes bibliographical references and index.
  ISBN 978-1-63265-007-8 (paperback) -- ISBN 978-1-63265-991-0 (ebook) 1. Women executives. 2. Leadership. 3. Executive ability. I. Title.

  HD6054.3.M58 2015
  658.4'092082--dc23

                                                        2015027782

ACKNOWLEDGMENTS

I thank all the executive women and men who welcomed me into their offices and shared their stories of challenge and triumph with me. You taught me so much about the very best ways of leading. You may recognize yourselves in these pages, though I hope no one else will!

I am grateful to the senior executive woman who inspired my research 25 years ago, by saying, "Women have to walk a fine line here." You started me on a meaningful and rewarding quest.

I also thank Talent Strategy Partners' editor Anne Dubuisson for teaching me and leading me to discover my non-academic voice. By writing this book with her challenges and reinforcement, I saw my data in new ways and went through a self-development process of my own. It was a journey I will always treasure.

I give special thanks to Annie McKee, for her review of this book and her enthusiastic support. She not only read this book, she digested it and told me about her interpretations and personal insights that she gained as a result. I hold her in highest regard, and it is with the utmost admiration that I say thank you!

To all my colleagues who have encouraged me to write and pursue publication of this book, and there are many of you, I am very grateful. I particularly thank Andie Kaelin, Debbi Bromley, and Karen Basile for the many conversations that helped me crystallize the unique essence and theme of this book.

I thank my colleague Steve Heinen, who shared his continuing research on leadership competencies and brought new insights to the interpretation of the Women's Leadership Blueprint. And I also thank Mike O'Malley for his help and advice throughout this process.

I especially thank my business partner, Pat Schaeffer. She convinced me to write this book and gave me the resources, time, and space to do it. I can't thank her enough for giving me her perpetual support, optimism, and encouragement. I am so lucky to have such a wonderful business partner.

Also, I am so grateful to my husband, Ken, and son, Patrick, who put up with me tiptoeing off to my "book cave" to write, not just during the week, but also on vacations and weekends. And I give my particular thanks to Ken for his suggestions, his understanding, his emotional support, and his humor!

CONTENTS

Part Three: Using the Road Map
to Develop Leaders

FOREWORD

It's not often that a book brings outstanding research together with absolute practicality. Carol Mitchell has written just such a book—and on a topic we simply *must* attend to: women's leadership. Many people shy away from this important topic, or are quite frankly scared to take it on. Not Carol Mitchell. In *Breaking Through "BITCH,"* she helps us to understand why it is so hard for women to lead and succeed in our organizations today. Most importantly, she shows us how we can succeed, as leaders of today's organizations. And, while this book most definitely focuses on women's leadership, there are lessons here for all of us, men and women alike.

We all know that women leaders have very different challenges than our male colleagues. If this were not true, there would be more of us at the top. The reality is that it is very hard for women to succeed—really succeed— in most companies today. The problem is rooted in our societies' deeply held biases and prejudice, of course, and we need to continue to fight to change the fundamental unfairness we find in organizations all over the world. This will take dedication and *time*.

Meanwhile, what can female leaders do? How can we lead and succeed now, with the world the way it is?

In *Breaking Through "BITCH,"* Carol Mitchell makes a strong case for why women need to stop trying to be like men, and develop unique and different leadership skills that actually do help us succeed. Carol draws from her outstanding research to show us how women need to call upon their emotional intelligence and other skills that one might consider uniquely "feminine." In fact, this book shows us how women *must lead differently* than our male colleagues, and describes how to do it.

Breaking Through "BITCH" is a practical guide that explains what women need to understand and do to reach the highest levels in an organization and to succeed once we get there. This book is clear, it's actionable, *and* it's based on research conducted with executives. Carol lays out a road map for success, including a sophisticated competency model, portrayed with elegant simplicity.

Carol's road map for women's success gives us an opportunity to understand why we feel uncomfortable and pulled in so many directions when attempting to lead people. She gives women—and men—a sense of why it's so hard to lead as a woman, and why there are so many mixed reactions to our leadership—including the label so many strong women leaders have been given: "bitch." It's time for us to refuse the label, while staying strong!

What excites me most about this book is that it gives us an opportunity to visualize the kind of organizational cultures that we can create if we are deliberate and conscious in how we use our abilities and our competencies. While the world is no longer as much of a hierarchical place, and our organizations are not quite as authoritative as they once were, they are still pretty toxic places. *Breaking Through "BITCH"* points us in the direction of mutual understanding, respect, and collaboration. It offers a vision of an organization where there is more room for people to be who they are, support for people to be better than they are, and space for people to examine some of the cultural myths that we walk around with that are not helpful to anyone.

With the focus on a confidence that is not arrogance, a drive for achievement that is not destructive, a political savvy that is not cutthroat, a finely tuned radar to read our organizational environment, and yes, an emotional intelligence, we can all begin to create new and better kinds of organizations.

When you read *Breaking Through "BITCH,"* you will say "Oh yeah, that's true. Yeah, that's true, too" as you recognize yourself and your co-workers. And you will envision yourself, with Carol Mitchell's guidance, becoming the leader you wish to be.

—Annie McKee

INTRODUCTION

The Pennsylvania Conference for Women brimmed with over 7000 professionals from business, education and government. The stadium-sized hall seemed to vibrate with the excitement of a rock concert. Guest speakers; former Secretaries of State, Madeleine Albright and Hillary Clinton, former President of Wealth Management at Bank of America, Sallie Krawcheck, and former Delta Air Lines executive and host of the award winning television program "Judge Hatchett," Glenda Hatchett, shared their personal stories of setbacks and triumphs. Their messages were consistent, urging us to help women reach their dreams, and to make sure "all those ceilings crack for every girl and every woman here and around the world."

From my seat at table B1804, I joined in the passionate rallying cry, but later asked myself, "Why are we still talking about that glass ceiling?" While I understood from my own experience and the experiences of so many friends and colleagues on their journey to the C-suite, that those choice spots were not easy to achieve, the metaphor of a "ceiling," an impenetrable barrier still surprised me. It occurred to me that the discoveries I've made and the experiences of many women as they have advanced, provide the key, tools and strategy to breaking that barrier.

I talked with many women that day, and my PhD research—particularly my development of a women's leadership competency profile—was embraced with such enthusiasm that I was inspired. Actually I was more than inspired; I was thrilled. I started my work 14 years ago, and have continued to build upon it since then. Here I was, talking with women in their 20s, just breaking into their career stride, women in their 30s, 40s, 50s, who had truly come into their own, and women in their 60s who had a wealth of lessons learned, all captivated and truly surprised by what I had learned about what it takes to be successful, particularly in male dominated roles.

The origin of this book stemmed from my position early in my career, as an R&D scientist, when I spent a lot of time observing the few women who were principal investigators. They would mostly focus seriously on their work, not partaking in the juvenile antics that their male colleagues enjoyed. Their reward? Their seriousness was seen as officious arrogance. And I am ashamed to admit it now, but I also thought these talented senior level women were being "sticks in the mud" by not sharing in the fun. One woman chided me about going along with the guys' work diversions. What was so bad, I thought, about rocking along to the Yes classic, "Starship Trooper" which we blasted from our lab's sound system every Friday at 3 p.m.? I was young and it was fun; I embraced the irreverence and rebelliousness of it. But I could see that senior level women would not let their professional guard down; somehow they couldn't afford the luxury of being a little wild and crazy at work and still be viewed as a serious force in the company (as men were). But at the same time, by being professional and serious, they were seen as choosing not to be a part of the gang. As the years passed, I began to wonder what I could do to step into their shoes without being viewed so negatively. By being wild and crazy with the guys I would not be taken seriously; but by giving up the party life and being focused and more serious I would be seen as a conceited killjoy.

This question stayed with me as I went back to graduate school to broaden my understanding of group dynamics and gender issues, simultaneously leaving the lab to begin a career in HR. Yet again, the few women who had "made it" into director and VP level roles across my company were often viewed disparagingly! The hallway chatter by both men and women and performance reviews suggested that the women who took the bull by the horns and led assertively were "brutal," they "tried too hard," they were "not a team player," or all three! Unofficially, they were simply labeled "bitch."

I was lucky enough to have a broadly well-respected senior executive woman who was a guide and protector for me. Among her nuggets of wisdom was: "Women have to walk a fine line here." She said that she had to take a softer approach than she might otherwise take because she is a woman. But on a femininity scale of one to ten—with one being without a trace of femininity— this woman was certainly not tipping the scale; she was about a four. So assuming "softer" meant more feminine, how much "softer" of an approach did she mean? What was the right balance?

It became clear to me that gender differences, what male leaders and what female leaders could "get away with " was such an obvious double standard that I wanted to spell out for myself and others what those differences were. I wanted to develop a leadership competency model—a dictionary of success-associated behaviors— specifically for women. If I had that blueprint, I could share it and help other women become effective and respected leaders. I conducted in-depth behavioral event interviews with well-respected men and women from Fortune 100 companies, among others, male and female CEOs and a female CFO in the pharmaceutical industry, male and female CHROs in the chemical and telecom- munications industries, a male COO in the chemical industry, a male CEO in the utility industry, a female

CEO of a large nonprofit, a male EVP of a large ivy league university and a female SVP Marketing in the consumer products industry—to understand how women lead differently than men.

What I didn't expect to find was that the profile of behavioral characteristics associated with the successful women leaders I interviewed comprised tempering their leadership behaviors with some stereotypical female traits and behaviors. Yikes! Was I really going to report that women have to act, well, more like women? Is this what my protector/role model meant so many years ago when she said that women need a softer approach? I was stunned. In my years of graduate study, I had read that women have to think more like men, be more like men. For years, I saw some women leaders do their level best to be gender neutral or at least downplay their femininity.

However, when you take into account that the reason women leaders have to act differently than their male counterparts is because we have gender specific expectations of them, it isn't so surprising that women would demonstrate some stereotypical behaviors to meet those expectations. By "feminizing" competencies such as achievement drive, confidence, strategic control, and influence, and by tempering assertiveness, successful women are managing gender expectations; that is, they are balancing being a woman and being a leader. These, and the other competencies I describe in the Women's Leadership Blueprint™, are the way that executive women make their male counterparts, and the people they lead, more comfortable with them as leaders, and thereby achieve better results.

My dissertation was complete, but my quest continued. I wanted to learn more about what makes women successful. I interviewed a new crop of women leaders in high tech firms, in healthcare, in big box retail, in the chemical industry, and the Women's Leadership Blueprint has stood the test of time and vagaries of the new economy. This academic pursuit has come to life as it applies so readily for my own success, for my colleagues' success and as a tool for my company's work in leadership development and talent management.

This book is organized into three sections. The first section lays the groundwork for understanding why women in leadership require a different repertoire of behaviors by looking at the impact of gender stereotyping and the conflicting expectations we have of women and leaders. The second section focuses on the Women's Leadership Blueprint. Each of the nine competencies is defined, with behavioral examples and supporting excerpts from the stories I heard during the executive interviews. The third section discusses how the Women's Leadership Blueprint can be used for developing both men and women to lead companies in the new and emerging business environment and for overcoming some of the hurdles women continue to face in their journey of professional development.

It is my hope that this book will help women understand the profile of behaviors that has led to others' success, and to customize those behaviors as they hone their own leadership style. I also hope that this book gives men and women mentors a common language for coaching women in how to be more accepted as leaders, and therefore, more effective. Though we may still have that glass ceiling, it has been cracked; and the women who have cracked it provide a guide for all of us! Much of our success is in our own hands. I hope this book strengthens your resolve and your belief in yourself to join those women up there above the glass.

"We have all a better guide in ourselves, if we would attend to it, than any other person can be."

—JANE AUSTEN

PART ONE

Why a Different Road Map for Women in Leadership?

CHAPTER 1

What's Sex Got to Do With It: The Impact of Stereotypes

Don't all good leaders have similar qualities that make them effective? Haven't we had the conversation about the different styles of leadership and when best to use them? Why would there be a difference in how great male and female leaders lead? What's sex got to do with it? Well, when female leaders who exhibit traditional male behaviors, are labeled "bitch," the answer is "a lot."

Leadership Is Masculine

When we think of leaders, many of the images we conjure up are distinctly male. We have familiar phrases that reinforce the maleness of power and leadership:

manpower, the thinking man, fraternal order of police, statesman, forefathers, talking man-to-man, being man enough. The very lens that most people look through is a male one, often identifying leadership attributes in terms of sports or military imagery. A leader commands attention, doesn't pull punches, leads the troops, is a straight shooter. But that isn't so surprising when you consider what we expect of men in our society. It is virtually the same as what we expect of our leaders. In fact, it's easy to confuse leadership and masculinity. An effective leader is often admired for his command of the situation, his strength of character, for "being a man."

Masculinity is seen as consistent with powerful authoritative leadership, so much so that an ineffectual male leader is somehow seen as less of a man. The unspoken, or sometimes blatantly spoken, question is: "Is he man enough for the challenge?"

In a television advertisement, one male character taunts another male character who was not asserting himself by saying, "What, are you a girl?" In another commercial an adolescent boy calls another "an old lady" when he doesn't try a risky maneuver on his skateboard. A commercial depicting a football field practice shows a coach barking orders like a drill sergeant saying, "Come on, ladies." One could go on and on, but the trend here is evident.

Questioning the masculinity of leaders goes to show that traditional leadership behaviors are seen as "male." If he's not demonstrating these traditional behaviors he's not a man, or not "enough of a man." But the real problem here is that ineffectual leadership is then labeled as being female. This is continually reinforced through the media, and research also bears this out. In comparisons of how of gender and leadership are perceived, men are described similarly to how leaders are described. How women are described doesn't even come close.[1]

A male leader who is effective in the eyes of others is viewed as being more of a man. A man's sexual desirableness and male sexuality are associated with power. For heaven's sake, when a leader in business is courageous and "stands firm," we say he has balls! What is so tough about that part of the male anatomy? I am not even going to comment on "standing firm."

Men demonstrate that power physically, financially, and/or intellectually. Think about male figures idolized in our society: the man in uniform, be it military, police, firefighter, sports; the man who commands huge financial resources; the brilliant entrepreneur. These men that demonstrate mastery and power are seen as sexy.

So, for instance, effective leaders are "strong," "powerful," and "potent." Too often, masculine terms are used to mean good while feminine terms are used to mean bad. When I worked for a large firm, I received a copy of a memo summarizing our firm's financial results and utilization for the month. The memo was from finance to the head of U.S. operations. Bolded words are my own emphasis. The second paragraph read:

> Utilization at the consultant level (XX%) continues to be **strong** exceeding budget. Utilization for all remaining levels lags target. Partners' utilization has been **soft**, dropping to (XX%) for the month of July.

The memo intends to convey that the consultant level was doing well because their utilization (billable hours) was higher than what was budgeted, whereas the partners were not doing well because their utilization was lower than budgeted. The use of the word *strong* to mean good, and the word *soft* to mean bad is just one example of how we continue to perpetuate gender issues. Words become so much a part of a lexicon that we don't even realize, or at least we don't think about, what their underlying meaning might be.

Getting back to the aggravating memo, look at the word *soft*. It has many definitions in the dictionary; a representative few are:

- Marked by gentleness, kindness, or tenderness.
- Smooth.
- Lacking firmness or strength of character, feeble, unmanly.
- Having relatively low penetrating power.

The word *strong* also has many definitions; representative ones are:

- Having or marked by great physical power, robust.
- Having morale or intellectual power.
- Having great resources, wealth.
- Power derived from muscular vigor, large size, structural soundness.

Using the word *soft* to describe poor business results and *strong* to describe good results implies that poor results have a feminine quality whereas good results are masculine. And for heaven's

Using the word soft *to describe poor business results and* strong *to describe good results implies that poor results have a feminine quality whereas good results are masculine.*

sake, soft is described as having "low penetrating power." Need I say more?

The subtle association of leadership as male can creep in and be reinforced through images that are apparently beyond the conscious awareness of those in power. At a state-of-the-business meeting of a large management consulting firm, a presentation title slide bore the photo of the three top leaders posed at the end of the national mall, in front of the Washington Memorial. Of the 400 or so senior consultants in the room, only a handful of attendees chuckled at the fact that our pale male leaders where posing with perhaps the most prominent phallic symbol in the nation!

The Good Woman

So where does this leave women who want to lead? What are the images that come to mind when we think of women? Women can be seen in many different lights, but there are three female stereotypes that are reinforced and they feed into what we expect of women.

1. Woman as Nurturer

Women are caretakers of children, of elder parents, of the household. This image isn't reinforced as much today as it was in the sitcom days of Alice the maid on

The Brady Bunch, but the expectation of nurturing certainly continues to be reinforced through various media. Commercials and print advertisements show women using the furniture polish, heating up the frozen dinner, extolling the benefits of a particular disposable diaper, far more than they show men engaging in these tasks.

2. Woman as Seductress

Every generation has its icons of sexuality. Our cars, our household products, our vacation destinations, and our health and beauty products are marketed to us by sexually idealized women. Some are subtle; some of the ads are blatant.

I will never forget Super Bowl XLVI in 2012. We had a small group of friends and family (all men but me, as it turned out) gathered to watch the game, including my husband's boss, who was in town from the UK. There was a commercial by a Web hosting company that will remain nameless. The commercial featured a female model on a pedestal wearing a scant bikini being painted with marketing information of the company. Later in the game the same company had a second commercial showing women on a dry ice–fogged stage wearing, yes, scant bikinis, talking to two young men about making all their (internet) dreams come true. One of the women in a feathered wrap, with apparently nothing else on, stepped out front and center as the two guys said, "Is this heaven?" She said, "No, but this is" as she was apparently opening the wrap. The screen whited out with a bright "heavenly" light in time to hide the "reveal-ation."

Okay, that was extreme, but there were five other commercials with women in bikinis, with women seducing someone (sometimes the TV viewer), or both. Sex sells, and in our society, sex is women in scant clothing and women acting seductively. The Super Bowl is notorious for its extravagant and edgy commercials, of course, but it does show how men like to see women. I was embarrassed, but the men watching these subtle and not-so-subtle commercials didn't blink an eye. (Because they didn't want to miss anything?)

3. Woman as Saint

These are women who are put on a pedestal. Mother Teresa, Princess Diana, Grace Kelly, and Jackie Onassis fit into that quintessential beauty-radiating-from-within, regal, and pure image we like to associate with women. Think Galadriel, the elf queen of power and wisdom in *The Lord of the Rings*, played by Cate Blanchett, who actually glows with an ethereal light when on screen!

Because these stereotypes are so valued, and so promoted as the ideal, they continue to get reinforced even as women take on more and very different roles. Although men also struggle to fit some stereotypes for the ideal man, those stereotypes are not inconsistent with leadership as are the stereotypes of women. (Although perhaps an elf queen would make it to the C-suite.) Though feminine traits that emphasize warmth and expressiveness are highly valued in society, these traits are not generally associated with leadership and power.

The challenge for women in positions of leadership— or working toward positions of leadership—is that they have to deal with the fact that we first have expectations of them as women. We expect them to be interpersonally sensitive to us, to be supportive of us, to be inclusive and welcoming. These are not typically what we expect from our male leaders.

If a woman ignores the set of expectations we have of her as a woman and demonstrates behaviors associated with strong, competent leadership, she is frequently criticized. Her femininity or sexual orientation may be doubted. Her humanness, her normalcy, will be

The challenge for women in positions of leadership—or working toward positions of leadership—is that they have to deal with the fact that we first have expectations of them as women.

questioned. Her behavior will be viewed in exaggerated terms. We will see her as harsh, abrasive, aggressive—as in, "he's assertive; she's pushy." And yes, we will label her a "bitch."

The first female CEO in the auto industry went before the House and Senate to testify about her company's delay in recalling vehicles with defective ignition switches. A male colleague of mine watched some of her testimony and said she seemed unemotional and too defensive of her company. He said, "She didn't say, 'This is absolutely awful! We will do everything we can to fix this.'" I had to wonder if he would expect a male CEO to be "emotional."

Does She or Doesn't She?

The flip side of the coin is: What if a woman leader does demonstrate some of those behaviors we associate with women? Some research suggests that femininity has a negative effect on women's advancement and that "female managers should be cautious about demonstrating a feminine orientation that could reinforce perceptions of incompetency in the minds of organizational decision makers."[2] The perception that a "feminine orientation" means incompetency certainly puts women in a catch 22! Demonstrate nurturing, interpersonally sensitive behaviors so that you aren't a "bitch" but don't be too feminine, or you will be seen as a "ditz" or, worse yet, a sex object. Can't win for losing!

This unfortunate phenomenon happened to a female VP heading a staff function at a Fortune 100 company. She was smart, attractive, and confident. She was knowledgeable, charming, witty—everything that seemed to be associated with being a successful woman leader. She was seen as a star initially; however, colleagues' perceptions of her changed over time and their comments reverberated in hallways and offices behind her back. Some women were disparagingly referring to her as "Barbie," and many of the men had written her off as a socialite and flirt. The same set of behaviors that made her a star when she first came to the company later somehow clouded the fact that she was a competent contributor. Her behavior had not changed, but people's perceptions had. She had been admired for her relationship-building and interpersonal skills when she was new to the company; however, those behaviors were later seen as flirtatious. And although these behaviors got her hired into a top job, woe to the one who exhibits them once she is there! People "sexualized" her behavior so that she was seen more as a seductress than a competent corporate leader.

Interestingly, an executive coach told another woman I know, who was a VP in the very same company as "Barbie," that she should wear makeup and "flirt a little." Yes, the company had hired a coach for this VP because she was seen as just a bit too masculine. Like I said before, can't win for losing!

Back to the hazards of demonstrating femininity, I worked with Meredith, an EVP of HR for a financial services company who was in her late 30s, was in a rush to have a program design, and wanted something impressive and snazzy to present to the executive leadership team in three days' time. My female colleagues and I were facilitating a daylong meeting with Meredith and her three female directors to develop an outline for the program. The three directors "sided" with us in various debates that morning, and Meredith became more defensive as time went on. We took a break as lunch was brought into the conference room. Meredith left for about 15 minutes and when she returned she had on dark—almost black—blood-red lipstick (think *Rocky Horror Picture Show*)! I looked across the table at my colleagues. One had a raised eyebrow; the other was visibly forcing herself not to crack a smile. It was as if Meredith had put on war paint to intimidate us and reclaim her power over the team. She was used to being the "alpha female" in the room, so the present situation did not sit well with her.

The lipstick was just the icing on the cake, or lips. Meredith always sported high-fashion edgy clothes, shoes, bags, and accessories, exuding an air of high-wattage superiority. The in-your-face emphasis on her sexuality was amped up a notch or two or three when she felt threatened and was fighting for territory. Her subordinates and executive peers alike saw Meredith, no surprise, as a "bitch." She was asked to leave the company six months after our design meeting.

I've seen this aggressive posturing—amping up sexuality—in other meetings where the attendees were all women. Angela, a director for an insurance company who was in her mid-30s, entered the conference room of her peers 20 minutes after the meeting had started. She glided into the room, took a seat at the head of the table, dramatically peeled off her closely tailored suit jacket, and stated, theatrically and nonchalantly, "Sorry I'm late." As we continued our discussion, Angela sighed from time to time, tossed her head to swing her long glossy locks off her shoulders, and occasionally stuck out her chest as she repositioned herself in her seat. She didn't apply blood-red lipstick, but there was no question that she was throwing her sexuality out into this room of women in an assertion of her dominance.

After the meeting, Angela's peers caught up with my colleagues and me in the parking lot. One said, "Can you even believe her? She prances in like a princess and then interrupts the conversation with her sighs of boredom.

She thinks everyone is beneath her." Another woman said indignantly, "She sticks out her chest like she's going to overpower us with her oozing sex appeal. What's that about?" Yet another laughed and said, "She's just a rude, self-centered bitch!"

The expression of sexuality can be used as a lure or weapon. It can be perceived as desirable or hostile, too much or not enough. It speaks volumes, yet what is it saying?

The expression of sexuality can be used as a lure or weapon. It can be perceived as desirable or hostile, too much or not enough. It speaks volumes, yet what is it saying? It is an aspect of oneself that has to be considered carefully when operating professionally.

A very astute observation that an executive woman shared with me was about how she thought a female leader has to deal with sexuality:

"I feel that one of the things that's really tough about being a female executive is that there is a de-feminization that goes on as you advance to higher positions. You neutralize your femininity, but also, you are not treated as much as a woman as you would be if you were at some mid-level position. If you have any insecurity at all about your femininity, your sexuality, your level of attractiveness, it is really tough. People treat you like a man, or a houseplant, or whatever it is...."

The "Bitch" Barrier

Both executive men and women have told me that if women do not find that perfect balance of sex stereotypic behavior (femininity) and professional leadership behavior, they are judged more harshly. As one man put it:

> "Women have to be all the things white men are, minus the things we would judge women harshly for (*aka* behaviors that give them that scarlet "B"). Women have to know when to stop arguing a point, to not be demanding and never use foul language. She must have the best qualities of being a women, married with all the best qualities and safest qualities of being a man."

Powerful Women Are Masculine: She's No Lady

If we could expand our thinking about gender, a woman seen as "acting powerful" would *not* be seen as acting like a man (or acting like a "bitch"). But as it is now, we see two separate and "opposite" genders: feminine and masculine. You are either one or the other. However, it would be more accurate to see two separate spectrums, one for feminine and one for masculine, and to not associate them with a biological sex. Two separate spectrums allows us to talk about a combination of characteristics—some traditionally feminine, some traditionally masculine—that describe a person. Helen Fisher, a biological anthropology professor and researcher at Rutgers University, writes that each of us is a complex mix of feminine and masculine traits.[3]

An executive woman in a technology company, Beth, said to me, "People tell me, 'You're more like a man.' That's really not a nice thing to say. I'm not like a man. I'm a straight shooter; I tell it like it is and I joke around with people. I'm totally not intimidating." Her commanding position in her company and her assertiveness in standing up to other leaders, most of whom are men, naturally meant to some people that she was like a man. Beth gets that, but she doesn't back down. She told me a funny story about throwing a retirement party at her house for her boss, Jack:

"I have family pictures in frames on the wall. So during the party, Jack's looking at the pictures and he says to me, 'Which one of these is you?' Okay, so now some of the board members who are there start looking over his shoulder. Jack announces, 'This is Beth!' He's pointing to my brother! When I correct him, he says, 'I knew you were a tomboy!' I said to him, with some board members listening, "Hey, Jack, you know it's time to retire when you can't tell the difference between a boy and a girl." We all laughed; it's all good."

If you are a female demonstrating traits that are masculine (exercising power) it's like nails on a chalkboard. Sometimes it can be translated into something less jarring, something that diminishes the power of masculine-ness —like, as in Beth's case, being seen as a "tomboy," as in, playful, young, and scrappy.

The common reaction to women who demonstrate power overtly is to use masculinized epithets, conjuring up images of hostility. Other times it's simply translated as being a "bitch." It isn't unusual to hear a strong female leader referred to as "the dragon lady." Of course the famous "Iron Lady," also called "Attila the Hen," was used to refer to Margaret Thatcher. Hillary Clinton has been called, among other things, a "ball crusher."

Throughout history women in power have been vilified, often portrayed as murderous and over-sexed.

Cleopatra, in ancient Roman writings, was depicted as insatiable, treacherous, bloodthirsty, and power crazed.[4] Another female Egyptian ruler, Queen Hatshepsut, during her reign (c. 1500–1450 BCE), grew the wealth economy because of her astute focus on trade. But after her death, her male successor literally trashed her. He sullied her reputation and destroyed any physical evidence of her rule! In the eighth century CE, China's first and only female ruler, Wu Zetian, suffered the same character assassination. In addition to supposedly being vengeful and insatiably lustful, she allegedly murdered her son, her sister and her brothers, her mother, and her husband![5]

Throughout history women in power have been vilified, often portrayed as murderous and over-sexed.

Powerful Women Are Threatening: Fear of Lilith

In Jewish mythology Lilith is the Hebrew name of a female demon. The folklore is that Lilith was the first wife of Adam and, unlike Eve, was made at the same time and of the same earth as him. (It only took one of Adam's ribs to make Eve.) Lilith left Adam when she refused to be subservient to him. She has come to symbolize the quintessential "uppity woman"; standing up to and behaving aggressively toward men, she is someone to be feared.

Both men and women can feel a bit skittish of women in power. I studied group dynamics and psychology in graduate school, complete with the "Tavistock group[6]," also called the "T-group," experience (two and a half days, sitting in a circle with eight other graduate students, with no structure, no task, no leader, no fun) and a course called "The Power Lab" (two and a half days at a remote retreat camp with 23 other graduate students divided into three "social" groups: Elites, Ins, and Outs to create a "society" of people with different access to and control over resources[7]—yes, that means food and beds). I could write a whole book on those experiences alone! I learned about power: how it's given, how it's taken, how it's forfeited. And particularly I learned how women in power are perceived. These lessons have been reinforced for me over and over again in the "real world" outside of academia—as I have carelessly let myself get into difficult situations I should have seen and avoided!

In these different group settings, many participants were disturbed and anxious when a woman in the group took a leading role, particularly when it was early in the life of the group. Women were seen as manipulative and unsettling, and others would compete to displace her. In the Power Lab, when a small group of women secretly banded together to take over control of the society on day two, we actually feared violence and retribution!

The threat of women in power is rooted in a mythology of fearful female stereotypes, such as Lilith. And when a woman is in a leadership role where her authority is not well defined, she can be a victim of those subconscious fears. After all, in a vacuum, stereotypes like Lilith subconsciously creep in to fill the void[8], making a female leader someone to fight, or to run away from—figuratively, of course, not literally.

Powerful Women Are Manipulative: Beware the Cunning Woman

Traditionally women didn't have access to conventional avenues of power. They were encouraged to use their feminine charms and wiles to get their way. But that "traditional female strategy" to exert power is perceived as "covert or manipulative, as duping others and as behaving unfairly."[9] In the dictionary, *wiles* is defined as "devious or cunning strategies employed in manipulating or persuading someone to do what one wants." Some synonyms are *tricks, ruses, ploys, schemes, subterfuges, guile,* and *craftiness. Wiles* seems to be uniquely associated with women—with devious, cunning women. And these women play with one's emotions as a ploy to get what they want. They use ruses to deceive; they are not to be believed! This unfavorable concept of women with power is as old as dirt, but unfortunately, you can never really get rid of all the dirt!

So turn the clocks forward, and women do have access to conventional avenues of power. But when women are in power, they often still can be perceived as manipulative and underhanded, and therefore not trusted. This is a tricky issue because in order for women to be accepted as leaders, they have to temper any bold, in-your-face use of power, and therefore hazard being seen as less transparent and forthright, as will be discussed in length through these pages.

Nothing Kills Advancement Like Stereotypes

Many researchers consider stereotypes to be a major force impacting a woman's ability to advance in an organizational setting.[10] There are four conditions, inevitably present in organizations, that particularly facilitate stereotyping and the biased decision making that it produces.

First, when there are few women in leadership roles, the likelihood that stereotypes will come into play increases. This is true for anyone who is a minority.

Second, when people don't have good information on how results were achieved, they tend to interpret them to conform to stereotypes, particularly the one that women have less capability than men. The more inference that is required to evaluate performance, the more stereotype-based biases creep in.[11]

Third, when criteria for measuring performance—which leads to pay raises and promotions—are not well defined, evaluations become subjective. When subjectivity is involved in decisions about performance, pay and promotions stereotyped biases sneak in.[12]

Fourth, the use of stereotypes increases when performance cannot be unequivocally attributed to one individual. A woman's success is often explained away by factors other than skill[13], such as luck or hard work; other times it is attributed to someone else entirely. (How many times does a woman say something in a meeting and no one acknowledges it, and then 10 minutes later a man says the same thing and *he* has made a great point?) Attributing good work to someone else is particularly relevant given the emphasis on teams in organizations. Teams obscure the visibility of individual contributions and evaluations of individuals.

So these stereotypes are old as dirt, and dirt is very hard to get rid of. Where does that leave us? How do women who break through female stereotypes to become leaders, break through that barrier of "bitch"? It's like walking a tightrope, or as the executive woman that I mentioned earlier told me, "Women have to walk a fine line here."

So, what's sex got to do with it? Everything!

CHAPTER 2

How to Look Like a "Bitch" Without Even Trying: A Case Study

"A women leader is likely to be sent conflicting messages about how members expect her to behave (leader like, but feminine) and since many of these are incompatible, her inability to meet all these expectations can lead to dissatisfaction with her performance."
—RESEARCHER B.G. REED, 1983[1]

"Gender stereotypes contain imperatives, which reflect how people believe that men and women 'should be' and importantly, how they 'should not be.' In other words, a set of gender rules dictates how men and women 'ought to' behave, acting as a straitjacket that limits acceptable behaviors for both genders."
—RESEARCHERS C.A. PHELAN AND L.A. RUDMAN, 2010[2]

The study of women's leadership—what works, what doesn't work, and why—has been discussed for more than 30 years! Research on this topic persists and the non-academic presses are still a-flutter today with all the questions about why women leaders succeed or do not.

Buried in the academic literature, to which many women do not have access, is a simple message: Women have to balance behaving "leader like, but feminine." The purpose of this book is to illuminate this academic information in a user-friendly way, and to bring to the party a wealth of experiences from women leaders.

Women have to balance behaving "leader like, but feminine."

Throughout this book, I use stories to demonstrate what kinds of behavior work to propel women leaders through the "bitch barrier" to success. But to start out, I think it would be useful to tell a story that illustrates what decidedly does not work.

The story is about a female leader in a meeting. The team that was meeting was a part of the newly "slimmed-down" human resources department of the organization. The entire company had recently gone through a massive restructuring that resulted in a reorganization plan that required only half of the employees who were on the rolls at that time. Employees who did not fit into the new organization plan were listed as "redundant" and laid off.

Two people headed the team as co-directors: Frank, a white male in his mid-40s, who had served in an HR role for the majority of his 20 years in the company; and Samantha (who always went by Sam), a white female in her mid-30s, who was hired two years earlier. Sam is the star of our story.

The HR team represented a culture change that was particularly difficult. In the team were three former directors, all men, who lost their director status because of the reorganization. Marie, the one woman who had been a director, left the company because of the unconventional HR reorganization. The non-director team members were three women.

The setting of our story is a weekly meeting that Sam and Frank organized for their team to review progress on various projects. These meetings were structured such that Frank led one half of the meeting and Sam led one half.

Non-Verbal Actions Speak Louder Than Words

The meeting participants began to file in, picking up muffins and bagels that were laid out in the center of the conference table. They chatted about recent vacations.

Gradually they began to find seats and open their notebooks. All the while, Sam was quietly taking notes, sitting at the end of the table. Frank signaled the official opening of the meeting with "Shall we begin?" then announced Marie's resignation and her acceptance of a "great opportunity" as a VP in another company. There was a lively discussion about having a party and getting a cake, and then the air seemed to be sucked from the room as one of the women in attendance, a 34 year old manager, Sharon, leaned in and tentatively asked, "Are we going to...look to....um...." Frank looked at Sam knowing exactly what Sharon was about to ask. Sam looked at her notebook. Sharon continued, "Replace... Marie? Are we going to get another body?"

Non-verbal actions speak louder than words

The whole behavior of the team shifted from its initial "getting situated and comfortable" mode to a tense, more cautious mode. People lowered their voices, talked slower, with mid-sentence, silent pauses. It seemed as if everyone forgot how to speak.

Frank continued looking at Sam as if he was seeking permission from her to answer the question. As the seconds wore on, and Frank wasn't getting what he was looking for, he began to answer Sharon's question with an elongated "Ahhmmmmm." People in the team looked from Frank to the floor.

Frank continued to struggle, Sam continued to gaze into her notebook, and then Frank nodded his head in a slow "yes" motion and said, "I think that would..."—he leaned far back in his chair with another unsuccessful attempt to catch Sam's eye—"...that would be helpful."

Everyone in the team laughed, except Sam. All eyes moved to her as the team awaited her response. The relieved laugh turned to anxious throat-clearing and shuffling of papers. Why wasn't Sam saying anything?

As if there weren't enough tension, Sharon added another hot potato to the basket. "Well one of the pieces of news that I heard this morning"—she hesitated— "was that Roger was made redundant." (Roger was a widely beloved HR guy.) Everyone looked expectantly at Frank again.

Sam finally spoke—for the first time in the meeting— before actually looking up from her notebook. She said, as if correcting Sharon's statement, "Eleven people were made redundant last week." Then she casually put the cap on her pen, not making eye contact with anyone.

One of the other women named another person who was laid off, to which Frank affirmed with, "Uh-huh." Sam, eyes still on that notebook, added in a flat terse tone, "Plus nine other people."

Sharon turned to acknowledge Sam's statement, then immediately turned to Frank to pose her question, "Would any of those people be—?" Then Patty, a woman who had not spoken in the meeting yet, quietly but audibly whispered to the person next to her, "It's not the people we want, though." A few people at the table smiled knowingly, acknowledging that the "redundant" people were not good candidates to join their team; the team wasn't going to "rescue" them from being laid off.

Frank replied to the question that Sharon didn't finish, saying, "I don't know." With that Sam came alive. "No!!" she exclaimed in a low voice. Well, that got everyone's attention. She wasn't finished. "No" she said again, this time louder. Then making pointed eye contact with Frank she let forth a third and final "no" just for good measure. Ouch! A still silence fell on the team; Frank and Sam maintained eye contact (oh, if looks could kill) for several long uncomfortable moments before Sam looked down. Others' attention scattered, most looking down. It was as if people had mentally skittered out of the room (like roaches when the light turns on) to get away from the discomfort.

Frank cleared his throat and moved on: "Ahum... okay...next." He looked at Patty, who was the project manager, for the next agenda item. Patty said, "Well, we'll just take the lead then." Sam was the only one in the team who laughed at the irony of Patty's pun about taking the lead. She must have thought the leadership vacuum in the team was hilarious.

It was then Sam's turn to take over the second half of the meeting. Clearly, her agenda was to directly address hard issues that her co-director, Frank, dropped the ball on. After 15 minutes of discussion on two agenda items, Sam brought up the failure of a project that had been assigned to two team members who were former directors. It began to get tense around the table as Sam confronted the team members, holding them accountable for not meeting their goal. Frank immediately came to the rescue saying, "We only failed if we failed to learn." Thank you, Mr. Comfort.

Sam then expressed her concern that some team behaviors were sabotaging other work. Frank repackaged her remarks by smoothly lecturing about the merits of making mistakes early while the stakes were not as high. Thank you again, Mr. Comfort.

The end of the meeting turned into an emotional rollercoaster ride, with Sam bringing up uncomfortable issues and Frank smoothing things over. Sam's final "bomb" was her disclosure that team members had told her that others on the team would not work for Patty on her project because of her former status as a secretary.

Two other former secretaries on the team admitted that they also felt that their former level was an obstacle.

Frank apologized to the women and assured them that he did not see them in a secretarial role. As Frank was smoothing and easing, Sam contradicted him, pointing out that he had given a project to one of the former secretaries that was really just answering phone calls and scheduling people for a seminar series. Frank tried to interrupt her by saying, "Wait...wait...wait..." As Sam persisted with her description of the menial nature of the task he had delegated to the former secretary, ("Book conference rooms A, B C and 7. Check with Janet on whether Bob can help set up AV equipment. E-mail invitations to the 87 people who should attend.") Frank raised his voice above hers, saying, "Wait...WAIT." Sam stopped her monotonic listing of tedious tasks, then sat there solemnly like a statue. Frank then said, "We've run out of time, but let's pick up this discussion about roles and projects when we meet next Tuesday. The room is booked from 8:30 to 11." This time people really did skitter out of the room like light-shocked roaches.

Two months after this meeting, Sam was terminated for "performance reasons." A senior leader in the organization said, "She was a cancer in the organization and had to be cut out." (A cancer, no less that needed to be cut out! It made being made redundant sound downright agreeable.) Others claimed that she just didn't fit the culture.

Four Easy Ways to Build the Brick Wall of "Bitch"

So who can tell me all the factors that made Sam look unapproachable, uncaring, and harsh? What signaled that she wasn't fit to be a leader? Was it what she said? Was it what she didn't say?

1. Frank's Lack of Directness or Decisiveness

The first part of the meeting could be called "Where's the Leader?" Frank's not taking control signaled confusion over the team's leadership. His hesitation was palpable, and the team's discomfort showed mostly in non-verbal ways.

Interestingly, it was the men on the team who had the strongest reaction to Frank's apparent lack of leadership. Two of the male team members actually brought their hands to their mouths, as Frank was struggling to get words out of his own mouth!

When Frank looked to Sam for help when he was in the hot seat, she refused it, making her look uncaring. His constant glances at Sam were, in effect, a deferral to her; and she was, in effect, rejecting him. She refused to "help" dissipate the discomfort and tension.

Frank's lack of willingness to play the traditional male leadership role served as a very bright spotlight on Sam's lack of willingness to play the traditional female role and come to the aid of her struggling co-director. That spotlight made Sam look harsh, almost hostile next to the poor fumbling Frank.

2. Sam's Lack of Affect

Sam didn't respond to cues from the team; she appeared dismissive. It was as if she were distancing herself from the proceedings. She avoided eye contact with the struggling Frank and with the questioning Sharon, mostly looking down at her notebook. She didn't laugh along with the team. She did not relieve their tension, as a woman leader might be expected to do.

When Sam did speak early in the meeting, she was monotonic, saying "no" (three times, no less!) to rescuing someone who was laid off—someone who was loved by most everyone. She spoke flatly as she made the point that other people had been laid off, too. (In other words, "Don't make such a big deal over Roger; he's one of many.") Sam's lack of affect and lack of inflection when she spoke had a chilling effect on the team. And indeed, she appeared to be "cold."

3. Sam's Directness

Sam did not sugarcoat anything she said, to say the least. She was not going to address the issue of bringing onto the team a person who had been laid off. She did not talk about why she didn't want to do that, or ask why others thought it should be considered. She simply shut down conversation. Sam was having no part of this nonsense about rescuing laid off people and not sticking to the serious business of the team. Her answer, unilaterally, was "no!" If Frank was not going to put his foot down and keep this team focused and productive, if he was going to play host to a coffee klatch, she would put her own foot down and keep things on track. Her directness, particularly in this meeting dynamic with Frank, made her look more like a strict school principal than a team leader.

4. Sam Being the "Bad Cop"

Sam repeatedly lobbed uncomfortable, but necessary, topics into the conversation, and Frank smoothed them over and minimized them. According to typical gender expectations, Sam would be a unifying, calming effect in the meeting, not a divisive, unsettling force. The fact that she behaved in exactly the opposite way was a big problem. But the most damning thing was that her male co-director appeared to be trying to make up for that, which exacerbated the team's negative perception of

Sam. Frank was trying to take on the traditional female leader role.

Sam not only failed to soothe and accommodate, she confronted issues head-on. Although this might have been perceived as a positive, no-nonsense style if demonstrated by a man, when demonstrated by a woman, it was perceived negatively. In this situation, it made her look like the quintessential "bitch."

Because I was regularly on site as a consultant, I heard the hallway chatter. Various team members described Sam as hostile and confrontational both before and after this meeting. They saw her as overbearing, having unrealistic expectations of people, and then giving them a cold shoulder when they didn't perform up to her standards. She had a very quick pace in a very slow, methodical culture. In talking with Sam, she told me she never really felt welcomed and supported as a new person in the company. She knew that her direct, results-driven style wasn't what people in the company were used to— but she was on a personal mission to get them into shape. She said, "Nothing ever gets done around here. It's like moving elephants down a very narrow hallway."

What's a woman to do?

So now we have a clear picture of what we mean by facing that brick wall of "bitch." Let's talk about how women are breaking through it.

PART TWO

Defining the Road Map

CHAPTER 3

Women's Road Map for Leadership: A Primer

It's easy to see why women leaders have to behave differently than their male counterparts in order to be effective. As discussed in the previous chapters, the characteristics of traditional leadership fit male, not female, stereotypes. The stereotyped concepts of "woman" and of "leader" are quite different. Behaviors expected of leaders are viewed as "role-discrepant" when exhibited by women and are perceived more negatively than the same behaviors when exhibited by men.[1] In other words, women who demonstrate male-stereotype leadership characteristics hazard being labeled "bitch," as we saw displayed so blatantly in the case study in the previous chapter.

Women must demonstrate leadership in a way that bridges the expectations we have of them as women and the expectations we have of leaders. Generally, women build that bridge by demonstrating a democratic and interpersonally oriented leadership style.[2]

Women must demonstrate leadership in a way that bridges the expectations we have of them as women and the expectations we have of leaders.

But what are the specifics of that bridge? What are the behaviors that cause a woman to be seen as a democratic and interpersonally oriented leader? How can a woman demonstrate the behaviors associated with effective male leaders without being seen as a "bitch"?

I have interviewed women in the C-suite and worked with countless others to identify a specific set of characteristics and behaviors that: define a successful executive woman, describe what she did to get where she is, allowed her to be a more democratic and interpersonally oriented leader, and indeed let her break through the brick wall of "bitch" to be seen as an effective and likeable leader.

What surprised me about my findings? I discovered an unmistakable theme. The truth is that executive women temper their leadership behaviors with some stereotypical female traits and behaviors! The women included in the research varied in their level of expression of femininity and their sexual orientation; they varied in personality type; yet the behavioral theme was the same. These women are being women: assertive, yes; driving, yes; in control, yes; but they have filed smooth the hard edges associated with stereotypical male leadership.

But 20-plus years of consulting with organizations on their culture, and the leadership characteristics that will drive their culture, has taught me that *one size does not fit all*. The Women's Leadership Blueprint™ is generic. The profile is a composite based on executive women from different organizations, from different industries, and in different jobs. So these behaviors may not tell the whole story for every setting or circumstance. Different cultures require different leaders. But the Women's Leadership Blueprint certainly reveals how women have adapted leadership behaviors and successfully advanced to the executive level of their organizations, regardless of industry, company, or functional area. This is how women are breaking through "bitch."

Women's Leadership Blueprint™

There are nine key competencies that successful women leaders embody, which I will describe in detail in the chapters ahead. Following is a brief description of each competency and how it allows successful women to break through "bitch."

Achievement Drive

Successful executive women are driven to do more or better than their peers and higher-ups expect. They set high standards for themselves, striving to accomplish unusual challenges. They seek out opportunities to achieve more than has ever been done. They do this in such a way that they are not seen as competitive and hard on their teams.

Conceptual Thinking

Executive women can see relationships and connections among seemingly unrelated pieces of information. They draw parallels and translate complex information into basic terms, "telling the story." They offer their insights so others understand, in a way that they aren't blown away or intimidated.

Confidence

Successful female leaders have a strong belief in their ability, taking on challenges with enthusiasm. They take smart risks, "stepping up to the plate" in tough situations. They exercise their authority, by sharing power with others, rather than stridently and independently enforcing their position of command.

Cultural and Political Savvy

Successful executive women see the cues and nuances of culture and group dynamics, adapting to work most effectively within the system rather than posturing to advance their own political power and status.

> *Successful female leaders have a strong belief in their ability, taking on challenges with enthusiasm.*

Inspiring Commitment

Successful female leaders create a company atmosphere of excitement, engendering a sense of belonging and loyalty. They get groups of people to buy in to the company or a team project, being solicitous of others' opinions and building relationships with and among others.

Persuasion

Successful executive women find ways to connect to the core values and passion of the person or company they are working to influence. Using empathy, women are able to sway people in positions of power in a way that doesn't threaten their power. They position themselves as a collaborator in accomplishing something together that they both want.

Self-Development Savvy

Successful executive women ensure that they get the appropriate developmental experiences and exposure in order to advance. They are proactive about managing their progression, taking positions that are stepping-stones to their career goals, avoiding those that could be "dead ends," and finding mentors and sponsors. Successful women take ownership of their career growth, rather than being bitter about a system that impedes them or at least doesn't help them.

Strategic Control

Successful women leaders steer critical initiatives by delegating to and empowering others, while maintaining control. They focus others on understanding and achieving exactly what they want to achieve and how they want to achieve it. In this way, executive women are in charge but are perceived as being collaborative.

Tempering Assertiveness

Successful executive women take the edge off their assertiveness through humor, empathy, establishing common ground, and building rapport. By doing this, they put others at ease, creating a sense of relatability and approachability.

The behaviors in the Women's Leadership Blueprint work in unison to achieve the desired result of breaking through "bitch." The strident ambition of achievement drive, confidence, and strategic control blend with the engaging egalitarian-ness of tempering assertiveness and inspiring commitment. The intimidating brilliance of conceptual thinking blends with the ability to connect and adapt, essential to persuasion, cultural and political savvy, and self-development savvy.

The Women's Leadership Blueprint is consistent with what one would expect among all successful executives[3]—that is, striving to achieve the best, showing confidence, effectively influencing others, leveraging cognitive ability, and having awareness of—and compensation for—organizational politics. Executives that I have interviewed demonstrate most of these competencies at some level, but women demonstrated them differently than men. And *that* difference makes *all* the difference.

In the following chapters, the details on *how* and *why* women demonstrate these competencies differently than men are revealed through the stories and words of the executives I interviewed.

Tighter Bounds for Women Leaders

When I interviewed executives I noticed that men demonstrated a broader range of behaviors than women. Although men had some behaviors in common, there were those that were uniquely associated with each man. Women had far more characteristics in common, indicating a more compact portfolio of leadership behaviors.

This is a fairly well-known phenomenon, and research has shown that women indeed often operate within a narrow band of acceptable behavior.[4] At a women's conference I attended, Madeline Albright said, "We all know that the range of behavior that men can get away with is"—she stretched out her arms full spread like she was showing the size of a huge game fish she'd caught—"and the range that women can get away with"—she brought in her arms in so her hands were about a foot apart. And though she didn't say that the reason women can't get away with as many behaviors is that they risk being labeled "bitch" and not succeeding, among the thousands of women in the audience, there were a lot of nodding heads and knowing smiles.

One male CEO said, "Women (in leadership) have to be everything that a white male expects a woman to be so he can be comfortable. She also has to be all the things white men (in leadership) are, minus the things we would judge women harshly for." That, of course, whittles down women leaders' choice of acceptable behaviors! There just isn't much overlap between "acting like a woman" and "acting like a leader."

So, why the similarity in the women's behavioral portfolio? Are organizations more accepting of a wider range of behaviors from executive men (that is, they let them get away with more) than from executive women? No question there! Do women need a specific set of behavioral competencies to lead successfully while men do not? Surely! Do only women with a narrower range of behavioral competencies pursue these executive positions? Really?! Is this lack of diversity among executive women due to organizational selection or self-selection? Who knows? But I suspect that women would hazard an educated guess that our organizations filter out the women who go beyond the acceptable bounds, putting them behind the brick wall of "bitch."

The competencies in the Women's Leadership Blueprint have stood the test of time and scrutiny. Over and over women of all ages, at all levels of leadership, in non-profits and for profits, in the public and private sectors, have confirmed their validity. They are echoed in headlines, articles, and academic studies about how women leaders' are perceived, how they succeed, and how they fail. Finally, what the Women's Leadership Blueprint provides is a full picture-window view—not just a porthole glimpse—of what successful executive women do to be effective leaders. What do they do? They manage gender expectations and in doing so, they break through "bitch."

CHAPTER 4

Step Up and Hit it Out of the Park: Confidence and Achievement Drive

---

Belief in oneself and the drive to accomplish more and achieve better results go hand in hand. Only with confidence in her knowledge and abilities can a woman compete with higher-ups and reach the brass ring. Both competencies—confidence and achievement drive—have the markings of assertiveness, competitiveness, independence, and masterfulness—that is, those characteristics that fit the male, not the female, stereotype. Successful women leaders have rounded off the edge of these male-associated characteristics, creating versions of their own and breaking through "bitch."

Confidence

Janet, the senior VP at a technology company, exudes energy and competence. She is a breath of fresh air. With her bright, makeup-free face, warm winning smile, crisp cotton shirt and perfectly tailored suit, it's as if she just walked off the page of a J.Crew catalog. This woman, who is not quite 40 years old, has the enthusiasm of a 20-year-old and the confidence of a well-seasoned professional. As an older colleague and friend of hers, I look at her with a bit of awe. She has managed to skyrocket to the upper echelons of a top technology company, seemingly encountering no barriers along the way.

When I interviewed Janet, I discovered, however, that what seemed like a cake walk to the top was occasionally a sprint over hot coals. After a successful eight years in the company, a former boss—and, how sad, a woman—told her that she was too blunt and there was "no way that anyone can be as confident." She proceeded to inform her that she had a fundamental personality flaw that must be the result of bad upbringing. (I kid you not.) Now, mind you, Janet was not disliked in this company— far from it. She had earned accolades and support from her peers and from those higher up who were in and outside her division. But this new boss of hers shook the solid foundation of my sparkling, confident friend. She started questioning herself and the company that she so firmly believed in. One woman systematically and single-handedly chipped away at a career's worth of positive reinforcement!

Consider the public debate that Sheryl Sandberg et al. raised in their "Ban Bossy" campaign. It seems—and we all know this—that even as children we are subject to being told to "pipe down," "keep your voice down," and stop "being so bossy." Whether the message is delivered by one adult in authority or a whole society of naysayers, it is clear: Being overconfident—and showing it—isn't lady-like, no one will like us, and therefore we will not be successful.

Confidence is a competency that shows up as critical in most leadership competency profiles. Belief in your skills, your judgment, and your personal brand is one of the more critical assets that an executive can possess. For a woman, though, confidence is fraught with peril. The example of Janet may have the additional complication of "women not helping other women because they feel threatened" but generally speaking, whether by women or men, by a boss or a person lower in the hierarchy, women who are strident, masterful, confident, and competitive are viewed negatively. They are not meeting our expectations that they be collaborative, and perhaps a bit self-deprecating. Women are not supposed to be that sure of themselves, as Janet's boss declared.

The Power of "We"

Despite these preconceived notions, executive women have found a way to be confident and competitive without raising the discomfort or disdain of their colleagues. What is their secret? They understand that confidence is about stepping up to the plate, about being self-assured; it's not about asserting one's authority. Although women do fully exercise the authority that is theirs, their confidence is often tempered by framing it as confidence in one's team or one's organization.

Although women do fully exercise the authority that is theirs, their confidence is often tempered by framing it as confidence in one's team or one's organization.

For example, one CEO of a pharmaceuticals company told me, in discussing her accomplishment of getting financial backing from Wall Street: "Not once did I feel unconfident about what we were doing. Never did I look back. We knew it was right. I think if we had put together a plan that we embellished just to sell to Wall Street that would have taken a lot of the joy out of it. We put together a plan that we believed in so much that it was easy for us to go out there and market it." When she tells this story today, she says,

"I just believed in what I was doing so much; I just did it." She advises, "Don't be afraid to speak up! Talent and smarts should rule the day." Her message is clear: If you believe in your company, stand up for it!

Another example of confidence—and chutzpah—comes from Paula, a CEO who talked about her efforts to license another company's technology. She said, "I just never remember thinking that it wouldn't work. It was more 'What do we need to get done? Here are all the things that we need to do.' I just kept focusing on that and was confident the results would follow." Paula fully embraced a belief and confidence in her company, and this propelled her to act confidently on its behalf. She's not just saying "we" because it softens the edge of her confidence or, more bluntly put, makes her less bossy; she says it because she truly believes the people around her and the company itself deserve the credit along with her.

Stepping Up to the Plate

So we've looked at the power of "we." Now let's look at another way in which confidence is demonstrated in a self-assured, "rising to the occasion" kind of way. Lauren, the CFO of a Fortune 50 company, is the type of person who speaks only when she has something to offer. Her MO is to listen. And as she was listening at a press conference with peers from her company and executives from the company with whom they were pursuing a joint venture, it became clear to her that she knew more about the details and the messaging than the spokespeople in front of the microphones. So, instead of ceding to her colleagues, she moved front and center to take over the responses to the press. She told me, "I made sure that there was no confusion about what the right answers were. The other people didn't know how to reply, quite honestly. Sometimes you don't wait on social niceties." But she did pay attention to "social niceties" as she spoke to the press. She stepped up to that microphone without stepping on toes, presenting herself as a part of the team and crediting her colleagues as she responded to questions.

As a point of comparison, Larry, a male COO, told me about his struggles to slog through a very politically constrained new construction project involving two entire city blocks. He had invested time in getting buy-in from various constituents in his organization. After meeting much resistance, he "drew the line": "I said, 'You know what, guys? I understand your objectives. Fine. They are registered. But, we're going to do it this way and that's it.'" Larry's assertive style—his absolute confidence in blatantly exerting his authority—is common among the executive men that I've interviewed. They can, and do, put their foot down. Perhaps more importantly, they seldom suffer the unfavorable consequences that women do when they stridently exercise their authority in the same manner.

Bill, another COO, demonstrated this assertive, no-nonsense approach in a different way at a meeting in which his peer presented a proposal he thought was ill-conceived. He said to the assembled executive team, "This is the proposal? This is not what we said we were going to be as a company! Reject this thing and let's move on to something else." I asked him at what point during the meeting he had said that. He said, "As soon as they started talking about it. I mean as soon as I saw them starting to go into this analytical mode, I said to them, 'This stuff—before we get into all this discussing the commas and semicolons in the proposal—this is not consistent with the corporate strategy we agreed to, so why are we even discussing this?'" Bill was standing down his peers in a very confrontational, challenging way. He was not just stepping up to the plate, as Lauren had done to take control in the earlier example; he was jumping up and down on it! Can you even imagine a woman getting away with delivering this message to her executive peers in this way?

Christine Lagarde, managing director of the International Monetary Fund (IMF), is a leader with a no-nonsense style, but she is assertive in a different manner than the male executives I interviewed. For example, she courageously presented at an annual Fed meeting in Jackson Hole that the European Central Bank (ECB) had essentially stuck its collective head in the sand about the global financial crisis. After the event, she described what happened from her perspective, saying, "I felt the necessity to publicly say, 'We are in a dangerous position. Austerity and deficit cutting is not the only panacea. We need to look at growth. Banks have to be stronger to be able to actually do their job, which is finance the economy.'"

She continued, "After my call to action, if you will, there was an element of resentment, an element of denial, and certainly very strong and vocal pushback about what I had said and a little bit about me, you know: 'Who is she to say that? How does she know, and who has informed her of such things?'"

Ms. Lagarde was not afraid to step up to the plate, lay out difficult truths, and call her colleagues to task, but she did it differently than the male COO did in the previous example. His approach was like a verbal whack on the knuckles, and confrontational. Ms. Lagarde offered what actions she thought needed to happen. She wasn't pointing a critical finger at anyone or claiming that they were doing it wrong; she was saying they could be doing more. And she didn't dictate, "You will do this, this, and this."

As a woman leader, she was in the difficult situation of having to assert her authority and expertise over her (male) colleagues and, naturally, she received some pushback—but as a result of her approach, she was able to effectively get the ECB to use unconventional monetary policies that were bolder in ambition and larger in scale (growth tactics). These exceptional actions helped the world pull back from the precipice of another Great Depression.

Women like Christine Lagarde are few and far between. Taking a top role governing a country or a multi-national organization means being at the top of a hierarchy. Executive women have talked about their distaste for hierarchy, so it's understandable that confidence doesn't look like asserting authority or mastery as it so often does with executive men. Women tend to distribute their authority, empower, and give credit to others. This is consistent with findings that women express a clear aversion to behavior that sets them apart from others in the company, that they have a distaste for "pulling rank."[1] One executive woman said to me that she preferred to think of herself as "first among equals." Another said, "Everybody is equally important; we just pay people differently because of the level of authority and execution that we expect."

This egalitarian perspective is welcoming and inclusive. It stands in direct contrast to the exclusionary and alienating atmosphere often created by emphasizing hierarchical differences. I suspect that executive women dislike hierarchy because it flies in the face of the inclusive style that has made them effective leaders. Playing down hierarchy has allowed these women to meet the gender expectations of those they lead. That is, they demonstrate a collaborative, democratic leadership style because it's what people expect and it works.

Sharing Power

Another way that women demonstrate confidence is by distributing power among their teams. When women leaders are collaborative, they have enjoyed better results and supportive, loyal followers.

At one time, people might have thought that collaborative leadership, which is sharing power, distributing decision-making, and casting a broad net to embrace leaders at all levels, was a way of side stepping taking the reins and forging the path. We had terms for it, such as *laissez-faire leadership*, to characterize it as unrestrictive, *loosey-goosey*, and *weak*. This cast a negative light on collaborative leadership. And because it is the type of leadership that women use in order to be effective, and is therefore most often associated with women, it diminished women leaders. The strong authoritarian leader who worked so well in hierarchical organizations was the admired model of leadership. That command and control leadership style was a model that advantaged men, as a man who is strong, commanding, and directive is seen positively. This is not true for women. Women cannot "get away with" this leadership style, much less be seen positively. Those who have tried are seen as overbearing and harsh.

Fortunately for women, and for companies as well, that authoritarian model has fallen to the wayside to be replaced by a more collaborative leadership style. It is what's needed in our current business environment. Collaborative leadership is no longer perceived as weak leadership—just the contrary. It requires leaders to have the strength and confidence to share power. At least part of the reason we need this kind of leadership now is that organizations are desperately seeking ways to create cultures that nurture innovation. It just so happens

Collaborative leadership is no longer perceived as weak leadership—just the contrary.

that sharing power profoundly and positively influences the culture, creating an atmosphere for ideas to form and flourish.

Terri Kelly, president and CEO of W.L. Gore & Associates, in talking about how to promote and maintain a culture of innovation, asks, "Are you ready to give up power to get results?"[2]

Giving up power is the courageous thing she actually did. To think that the very thing that women leaders do to manage gender expectations—that is, to distribute their authority and empower others—can be a driver of innovation! Gore is an unusual company in that they allow leaders to emerge rather than appoint them. So as a leader, "you aren't in a position to assume authority to *command* others" (my emphasis). Ms. Kelly inherited this model from the company's founder, Bill Gore. So it was not a woman who created this "lattice," non-hierarchical structure, but it certainly would seem to be the kind of structure where a woman can demonstrate confidence in a gender-consistent way, and not hazard the perils of asserting authority and commanding others. That sharing power drives innovation is evidenced by some interesting statistics. When Marissa Mayer became the CEO at Yahoo, there were 20 Fortune 500 CEOs who were women, five of them leading technology sector companies. This statistic is not surprising if you look at the culture of these companies, which emphasizes risk-taking and openness to ideas for the creation of new products, new markets, new customers, and new opportunities.

Some women leaders share power with the primary intention of engaging their team. This was true in the case of the head of regulatory affairs for a biopharmaceutical company. She told me about a particularly difficult case that she handled, getting FDA approval of a new biological compound while at the same time trying to solidify her team (that is, herding stray cats). She led a team of individuals, all of whom sat at the table presenting and discussing data with representatives of the FDA. She said, "I knew when we left the room, each of us would be walking away with our own version of what just happened. So I insisted that, as soon as the meeting was over, we have a debrief, no matter what time it is. We go back to the hotel, sit in a conference room and get all the facts out on the table. We didn't get to bed until 1 a.m." She made sure that each person gave their impressions, explaining that she didn't want anything out there in conflict with what the team agreed to report. Together, the team put together a document to bring back to the CEO. Doing this was good project management, but it was also an important mechanism for engaging her team. Although she was ultimately the one who was "in charge" and accountable for the quality of the effort, and the report back to the CEO, she distributed the power.

Yet another example of a woman leading through shared power is Marie, the CEO of a network of healthcare communication companies, who created a

100-percent employee-owned company. She said that she wanted employees to have control of their own destiny—to create a culture where everyone is an owner: "You know, it's capitalism with a socialist spin." (She winked and grinned.) Interestingly, when I asked her to describe her job as CEO, she said, "I oversee the well-being of the company. I am chief cultural officer, setting the tone. And I set the strategic direction of the company and represent the company externally." I couldn't help but notice that she put well-being and culture before strategic direction and being the external representative of the company. She truly felt that if she empowered the people in her company and created a culture that fostered ownership, she could point them in the right direction and get results. And they did.

Mary Barra, CEO of GM, is another leader from a very different industry and culture than the high tech-ish companies mentioned earlier, who believes that empowering people drives better outcomes. She has stated that "to win the hearts and minds of employees, we'll have better business results."[3] She has a bit of a different take on empowerment, saying that making people take accountability empowers them. The example she used was the 10-page dress code that she winnowed down to "dress appropriately." She thinks that people hide behind bureaucratic rules, saying, "I can trust you with $10 million of budget and supervising 20 people, but I can't trust you to dress appropriately, to figure that out?"

In peeling out bureaucracy and empowering people to think instead of following a detailed set of rules and procedures, Barra is in effect creating a culture that can nurture innovation. She is also creating an environment where she can lead without the confines and expectations of hierarchy shadowing her more democratic, inclusive leadership style.

All of these women have found a way to be confident and to gain the positive results of confidence—that is, to be accepted and welcomed by their bosses, peers, and subordinates. They believe in themselves, believe in their teams, believe in their company. And in most cases, they were able to assert themselves confidently without inducing the scorn of their colleagues—which brings me back to Janet, the young, vibrant, J.Crew-wearing SVP. After her boss dressed her down for being arrogant (too confident), Janet asked her for examples so that she could at least learn from them. Her boss said, "Oh, this is just my opinion of you." Janet's reply? " 'So if I'm hearing you right, you just don't care for me." She then reconsidered. "No, I'll take the feedback." Janet told other senior-level people in the company what her boss had said, asking if she really did impact others negatively; she did not. It turns out that boss of hers was known for saying these same things to some of the "strongest people on the team." Apparently, Janet's boss had a low tolerance for confident, capable women; yes, they were all women.

How does the story end? Janet's boss was fired within a year of being hired. Janet, on the other hand, continued to be promoted to bigger roles. She got something positive from that awful experience. Now she consciously monitors if she is being too direct and assertive for some people, and is ready to dial it down as needed.

Successful, confident women break through the brick wall of "bitch" by being inclusive and collaborative in their driving pursuits. They neutralize hierarchy, sharing power, framing their obvious self-confidence as confidence in the team, and crediting others.

Achievement Drive

Perhaps a more difficult competency for women to "get away with" is achievement drive. Oh, beware of the ambitious woman! Yet, achievement drive is the "fire in the belly," or the passion that drives incredible results. This is the competency that fuels competitiveness and persistence. Along with confidence, this is the competency that underlies risk-taking. Importantly, this is what feeds the will and the inspiration to execute business turnarounds. And it is business turnarounds that so often are the developmental grounds for emerging leaders to hone their leadership skills and gain visibility. Turnarounds are the proving grounds!

Women have not typically received these opportunities.[4] One male CEO told me, "The old boys' club is afraid to change from what they know works." His point was that women will do things differently, and in doing things differently things might not work as well as they did in the past.

Apparently, the board at Yahoo thought that Marissa Mayer might have a chance to turn the company around. And given the achievement drive she has demonstrated in the past, I think she has a good shot at it. She has said that her best decisions had two things in common: 1) She always chose to work with the smartest and most interesting people, and 2) She always did something that she was "a little not ready to do." It is the second point that gives us a clue to her achievement drive, her confidence and willingness to take risks. In a PBS/AOL-sponsored video[5], she said that when she took the job at Google, "the odds were fifty to one that we would fail." But she said, "If you push through that feeling of being scared, of taking a risk, really amazing things happen." She is attracted to un-navigated, unfamiliar territory, taking a risk on a startup that she thought had about a 2-percent chance of succeeding—a risk that paid off, as it turned out. She likes to learn, and learn fast. She was proud of being able to be a computer science teaching assistant in her senior year in college when, in her freshman year, a computer specialist had to show her how to turn on her new computer and how to use the mouse.

It's Not All About Me

Sue, an SVP of marketing in the consumer products industry, also spoke to me about taking on a challenge. She was in her job only eight months when the opportunity to take over the business unit came along. She said, "That to me was a very defining job, because it was a business that was in a great deal of trouble. It was losing a lot of money. It was either going to succeed or be shut down. To me, a great time to take over a job is when it's really messed up, because then you know whether you can do it or not." She saw this as a way to really test her abilities. But it had not escaped her attention that getting the business back together fed an ambition to get ahead. She said, "If you can turn it around, that will be a feather in your cap in terms of further up-line progression." She also couched the success as a team achievement, which we have seen so many women do in order to express ambition and achievement drive in a way that is acceptable, saying, "I did that, and I had a great group of people. We were fortunate in being able to turn it around." In the end, she did turn the business around and more: It became one of the best product areas in the company.

Fortune 50 CFO Lauren saw her accomplishment of initiating and driving a "hugely successful" two-year company merger and restructuring process as a high point in her career: "My counterpart and I had to really listen to each other, understand the needs, and work with our technical experts, tax expert, legal expert, pulling together big teams to help us. But basically I had to keep that process going to ultimate success." This was a pinnacle experience for her because it was "hugely complex," she "learned to negotiate," and she honed her influencing skills. At the conclusion of this demanding, exciting, "top priority" two-year process, Lauren said she felt a bit like she was going through postpartum depression. But, it wasn't long before she was looking for the next big mountain to climb.

For both Sue and Lauren, their passion to take on a big challenge involved rallying people, influencing people, and being highly interactive. This was particularly interesting in Lauren's case, as she is a self-described introvert, and has a personal, non-gregarious style of bringing people together. Both women found a way to make their "big hairy audacious goal (B-hag)" one that each member of her team embraced as their own. They demonstrate how achievement drive, ambition, and search for that adrenaline rush are mellowed by their ability to inspire commitment and engage others in their dream.

Competing Against Myself

Women demonstrate achievement drive as relentless desire to do one better or to do something none or few have done, or belief that one remarkable achievement isn't enough. For example, I have a friend who didn't stop at obtaining an MD, or becoming a general surgeon; she did a second residency in pediatric surgery. She told me at the time that there were quite a number of women surgeons, but she was one of a small number of women who were pediatric surgeons. Now she is known for some of the most complex fetal and neonatal surgeries. She chairs her department, practices, teaches, and does research at a major university health system. I think she's done it all, but knowing her, she will find something else to top her last greatest achievement.

For women, achievement drive is "to dream the impossible dream," to win, to be the best, to do something none or few have done. And when she is pursuing this dream with such passion, it tends to engage others rather than make them feel threatened or put off. Although men don't need to couch their drive to achieve as a noble pursuit of self-challenge, they aren't so different in their burning desire to be the best. One man explained to me why he pushed his authority to drive a project as "It [the project result] would end up being a B, a good B, a solid B, but I needed an A. I had to have an A."

Men also are proud of their extraordinary achievements, but they aren't as humble as women tend to be when they talk about them; men can take credit unabashedly. For example, a male executive, who wanted to encourage me about my career, took me to his office and pulled out of his top desk drawer (where the pens and pencils go) a well-worn sheet of paper with a hand-drawn graph. Across the bottom axis were years at the company; along vertical axis were salary dollars. He showed me the line tracking the rate of his increases in salary. He said, "When I started, I made X dollars. I was the one who opened the Louisville site. I was the one who got the Houston operations back on track. I'm now making Y dollars a year." I think his "career advice" was more about him showing off his achievements.

It brings to mind the phrase *proud as a peacock*. Is it any wonder why it is a male bird that is the chosen representative of pride? It also brings to mind all the discussions out there about women not bragging, not promoting themselves. As kids, being a show-off tended to be a bit more endearing when it was a boy doing the showing off. Girls weren't supposed to brag—and avoided bragging;

it looked too much like they were trying to "show up" someone else—not exactly a collaborative, power-sharing thing to do.

Achievement drive can focus on doing the undoable, surpassing expectations—even your own—and pushing to be the best. Some of the executive women that I've worked with seem to be on an endless quest to see just how high they can go. They remind me of one of my favorite tennis players (ironically a male), Rafael Nadal, who really is playing against himself. It isn't about beating his opponent. The person on the other side of the court provides him the opportunity to see how much more he can perfect his shots and his game. Oh, he wants to win, all right; he falls to the ground in relief and amazement when he's achieved another title. He joyfully runs the perimeter of the court lifting his trophy to the crowd. But you just know he's happy because he's proven to himself, one more time, that he is the best. And you also just know, he'll get back on the court in another tournament, in another match, and feel compelled to outplay his past best.

Executive men talk about surpassing expectations and doing the undoable, but it sometimes seems to be more about stoking their feeling of power than about drive to achieve more and better. One COO took pride in the fact that he had single-handedly influenced a three-billion-dollar decision. He said, "It took a lot of convincing. So, it was very refreshingly reassuring, exhilarating to have a company of this size make a three billion dollar investment basically on my say so." Another male executive told me about a sale that he led, saying, "Not only did we get approval but we sold bigger than everybody else thought we would." He also talked about getting funding when the market was not favorable. He commented, "Two years ago I raised $90 million of a straight equity offering when nobody was making any money at all. The market was pretty much closed. We had a different kind of strategy for identifying investors that hadn't been tried before." He then proudly described his strategy. "It worked out great. We made $90 million in four days. It really set us up."

In my interviews with male and female executives about their proudest accomplishments, I thought it was interesting that the men mostly talked about the acquisition or distribution of money. Although there was one female CEO who talked about getting funding from Wall Street, the main themes in the women's stories were about turning a business or business unit around. None of the men talked about business turnarounds. But business turnarounds are more markers of achievement than they are markers of power. Because men's achievement drive seems to be focused on gaining power, perhaps business turnarounds aren't what they think of when asked about their proudest achievement. Instead, they think of command of money; the more money you command, the more power you have. Perhaps women think of turning around a business as their proudest achievement because few women have had the opportunity and succeeded.

Women's achievement drive seems to be about pure achievement—never settling for less than they think is humanly possible. Power just isn't the ultimate goal for them. But because such women are so bent on getting higher, better, more, faster, do they even notice achievements that aren't at that top level? Do they appreciate the less-astounding accomplishments along the way?

Michelle, a senior executive leader of a global law firm who has won award after award, has personally driven the expansion of her firm, and has excelled in her practice area, when asked, "How did you do all this?" says, "What did I do? I didn't really do anything." I say to myself, "So... what? You didn't cure cancer or climb Mt. Everest?' It might be that she downplays the drive that pushed her to the top. But I got the impression that Michelle truly did not recognize her achievements as a big deal. She is still working toward whatever is that brass ring.

Women leaders demonstrate a relentless desire to achieve. They are ambitious, but not driving to gain power; instead, they are pursuing huge goals that will gain them visibility and satisfaction. And they are going after goals without being in hand-to-hand combat, competing with their peers. In fact, for many women, they are not focused on competing with others at all; they are competing with their own personal best, which does not threaten those around them. And in doing this, they break through "bitch."

The drive to achieve and the confidence to do what it takes to reach one's goals are critical for leaders. Women in leadership have the additional necessity to translate and modify these critical competencies to make them less threatening. The overarching themes for how they do this are collaboration and egalitarianism. The ability to do just that, as shown in example after example, is how successful female leaders get exceptional results and, of course, break through "bitch."

CHAPTER 5

Win Them Over: Influence

Influence is a vehicle to wield power without being blatant and women who are successful leaders use this in three different ways. They "persuade up" by establishing a shared vision, they inspire commitment by reaching out and engaging staff, and they steer critical initiatives by articulating a vision and collaborating with their delegates. Using inclusive behaviors to keep control, gain buy-in, and advance their agendas, women are sidestepping the "bitch" wall.

Studies show that executive women demonstrate influence skills more than their male peers, being a strength in 32 percent of women compared to 21 percent of men[1], indicating that this group of competencies is particularly important for women's leadership success.

They say the Irish have a hundred different words for *rain*—not surprising since rain in all its various nuances is such a prominent backdrop to their lives. My research shows that executive women similarly demonstrate several different nuances of influence. First, there is the influence that is demonstrated to persuade people who have more power than they do. Second, there is the influence that inspires the commitment and engagement of their peers and people with less power than they have. Third, there is the influence that guides the successful results of strategic initiatives that are delegated to others. Although these three aspects of influence are distinct, what they have in common for women is that they are exercised with finesse. It is finesse that balances meeting gender expectations and exercising power to advance agendas.

Type 1: Persuasion

Karen, the CEO of a biological sciences company, told me about a time when she convinced a smaller company to license its product to her company. In her research, she found that the inventor of the product had developed it for personal reasons and was therefore reluctant to turn over control. She also knew that the company would not enter the agreement without the inventor's approval. She recounted, "I knew that if we had a chance to talk with the inventor, and help him understand what our company is about and why we were the right partner, maybe we could progress the discussions."

She flew across the country to meet personally with the inventor. Karen recalled:

"We did a lot of work ahead of time to help him understand how we would position the product; why we were well-suited to do that; why this would be an important product for us; and, that unlike a very large company, we would treat this as our big product."

"This was his baby, and I wanted him to know that this was also our baby. It was a drug that he invented for his son who was suffering from a rare disease, which had the potential to fill an unmet medical need in the marketplace. These patients are suffering horribly, and this was about bringing hope to these patients. It was my job to convince him of that; that we weren't looking at it as just a commercial opportunity. I succeeded."

This example illustrates the "influence process" that basically involves three steps:

First, doing the research to understand the motives/values/goals of the person that one wants to influence.

Second, finding the connection between one's own motives/values/goals and theirs.

Third, telling stories that reinforce that connection.

This type of influence also illuminates how one cultivates a personal brand. Karen told stories to the inventor and his colleagues that illustrated and reinforced the mission and values of her company, and also reinforced what she stood for as an individual and a business leader. Executive women persuade by finding ways to connect their core values and passion with those of the person or company they are working to influence. In doing this, they are showing empathy, a quality that is highly valued and highly expected of women. This emotional intelligence files off the edges that could lead the recipient to feel overpowered in pursuit of an agreement. Sure, some might say that purposefully connecting to someone's emotions in order to persuade is manipulative. But when authentically discussing a shared passion, I would argue that it is not the "dark side" of emotional intelligence[2] at work; rather, it is managing gender expectations at work.

The art of persuasion is clearly seen in the nonprofit world, where resources are limited and directors have to lobby for program support within their organization.

Sandra, a VP of community health initiatives, saw that in order to address an addiction crisis, her department needed to restructure and align with the populations in need. She said, "Some people focus on the heroin epidemic and how to solve it, but that doesn't always address the root cause of the addiction and the best way to support people struggling with it."

Although Sandra knew Sam, the president, was very committed to going after the "true epidemic," their strategies for the approach and the allocation of resources were different. She said:

> "He felt strongly that we needed a consultant to come in and be with us full time to fully assess how we should address the epidemic because he thought my staff in the division of substance abuse had enough on their plates. So I had to build my case against that approach."
>
> "I said to Sam, 'If we are really going to redesign our system of care and how we support people who are living in recovery or struggling in addiction, the staff need to buy into it and lift it off. We've had consultants in the past helping us redesign. It took four years to the tune of 1.2 million dollars without it making the kind of change and impact we need.' So Sam said, 'I can see

you're very passionate about this and you know I feel very strongly about this, too.' He came around to seeing that we needed to do our own restructuring if we were going to have a positive impact in battling addiction. And of course, it freed up the budget money we would have used to pay the consultant."

Sandra knew that she could persuade her boss by bringing up their shared passion for making a positive impact in the addiction epidemic, but also their shared frustration with a past experience bringing in a consultant that didn't get to the root of the problem.

Both Sandra and Karen used an emotion-based connection to make a compelling pitch to effectively advance their agendas without being seen as too aggressive. Women using this approach don't threaten the greater power of the person they are trying to persuade. They are seen as a *collaborator* in accomplishing something that they *both* want. Executive women may be in a unique position to use this powerful way of persuading, because an "emotion-based" approach fits the stereotype for women but not for men.

Another example of this type of influence involves understanding the audience and tailoring ones approach to that audience. Brenda, the vice president of marketing for a consumer products company, was pitching a female-focused marketing strategy for a new company brand—Naturally Good—at their national sales meeting. She needed to convince the higher-ups that she had a good strategy and get their approval.

She started, "Well, the attendees were mostly all white, age 45-plus gentleman. So part of the challenge was talking about a marketing strategy for women in ways that they could understand. I had to talk about how this business—the brand and the market—was different than our company's biggest brand. I had to tailor, not necessarily the message, but how to convey it."

She continued, "So knowing that they would be skeptical, I began by telling some jokes. Then, I asked them to play a little game with me before I got into the presentation."

She described a game where four of the most well-known, good-humored "macho" men in the audience were held up as candidates to vote on for the "Naturally Good Playmate-of-the-Month," creating a parody of a beauty contest. The pictures of the four men—projected on the gigantic screen in the front of the auditorium—had been Photoshopped to don them in swimsuits and heels.

Brenda knew that the guys' paradigm for branding and marketing fit her new female-focused product about as well as the swimsuits and heels fit the four gentlemen in the Playmate contest. She said, "I made my point and it worked."

Brenda employed other methods as well to win over her audience. "Another thing I did very deliberately was to weave into my presentation examples of very successful companies that these guys hold in high esteem—that are doing a similar kind of female-focused nostalgia marketing, so that they had some evidence to believe that this was the way to go."

The power of persuasion is one of the most prevalent competencies demonstrated by both executive women and men, but there is a difference in how *they demonstrate it.*

Brenda succeeded by bridging the gap between her audience and her strategy. She found a nuanced way to bring along a group of middle-aged men into a world that was very different from theirs.

The power of persuasion is one of the most prevalent competencies demonstrated by both executive women and men, but there is a difference in *how* they demonstrate it. Executive women find and tie into an emotional connection to make their case more compelling. Men may use an emotional connection to convince others, but it is by working their established relationships, often one-on-one conversations in relaxed venues.

For instance, one executive man I spoke to described how he had anticipated obstacles in getting his senior leadership colleagues from other divisions to partner together. "So, I went around and talked to each of the leaders and I said, 'Here's what I'd like to do and here's why I'd like to do it.' Then I listened to their concerns."

The COO of a chemicals company always took the route of warming up constituents—often over dinner—to promote his ideas prior to a meeting. Referring to one situation, he said, "I went and met with each board member personally and explained my proposal to them. It was extremely important that I did it personally and privately. I wanted to allow them the opportunity to ask what they wouldn't ask in public. If you do it in public—at a full board meeting—and they have those questions but they wouldn't ask them, they might vote against it."

Although both men and women use facts and rationale to support their position, women are unique in that they also use a shared cause or value as the primary tool to persuade. By establishing an emotional connection in this way, as with so many other critical leadership competencies, women soften their aggressiveness and break through "bitch."

Type 2: Inspiring Commitment

Getting everyone "swimming in the same direction" is critical to the ongoing success of organizations. Much of that depends on a solid process of aligning goals up and down and across the organization. But in addition to aligned goals, people need to feel ownership and to feel an allegiance to the organization. This second type of influence is a way of engendering that.

Inspiring commitment is about getting buy-in, engendering loyalty and a sense of belonging among those in one's organization. Executive men tend to demonstrate this by creating an organizational community. They provide a forum for people throughout the company to hear about the business and ask questions, and, in providing this forum, they give people a shared sense of purpose. Men often create an image of a "winning team" beating the competition; and sometimes they create the notion of a common enemy to build loyalty and a sense of "we-ness." However, the motive and

Although both men and women use facts and rationale to support their position, women are unique in that they also use a shared cause or value as the primary tool to persuade.

rationale behind this is to maintain control of the organizational climate and ensure buy-in through continual
and consistent communication.

The male CEO of a biological sciences company
talked about how important it was to communicate to
employees. "I have a town meeting with everybody a
least once a quarter and I send a memo out every month
to update people on the kind of things that we're doing. I
want them to be up to date and know where we're heading. If they understand how their particular unit fits in
and what the strategy is, the employees get on board."

Executive women, on the other hand, engage people,
working to initiate and build on a collaboration between
themselves and those reporting to them, to inspire commitment. But it goes beyond just gaining cooperation.
Women leaders involve people in problem-solving and
setting goals, getting the buy-in of their teams, and
engendering feelings of ownership.

A CEO explained that her company was formed from
a business unit that spun off from a huge company and
from a management and administration team located on
two different sites:

> "You had a core of people in R&D who were
> hard workers and energized about the business,
> and through thick and thin they held on, never

knowing if they were going to have a job from year to year. I wanted to make sure they knew it was a new day. We gave out options to all the employees because we wanted to make sure everyone became an owner in the business. We had a huge party. We brought them together to meet their new colleagues and discuss our strategic plan."

Women leaders involve people in problem-solving and setting goals, getting the buy-in of their teams, and engendering feelings of ownership.

The CFO of a Fortune 50 company told me about involving her group in the process of addressing a significant issue. She recalled, "I'm sort of hitting them with a splash of cold water by telling them that the bottom line says we're going to lose ten million dollars this year and this is not acceptable. So now that I had everyone's attention, I told them that I didn't have the answer, but that I wanted to work with them to find it.' "

Another executive woman talked about setting up a special session to reengage her team after she had ousted a few "bad apples" from the group. People were relieved, but she realized that they still harbored frustration and didn't know how to change their group dynamics. She said, "We met to discuss how the team could be more effective. It was cathartic. I got great input from people, what they like, what they don't. They suggested what would make their jobs easier. Nothing was off the table. We even redesigned some of our processes to make the workflow more efficient."

Whereas women inspire commitment by setting up a two-way dynamic, inviting others' involvement, men essentially set up a one-way dynamic, influencing others to commit to him, the company, or the group goals. For executive women, the result of inspiring commitment is the establishment of an emotional bond among employees, as well as between employees and the executive woman. For executive men, on the other hand, the result is the establishment of trust—but not an emotional bond—between the employees and the executive man. It's less personal.

> *Whereas women inspire commitment by setting up a two-way dynamic, inviting others' involvement, men essentially set up a one-way dynamic, influencing others to commit to him, the company, or the group goals.*

The personal connections that executive women facilitate, the collaboration and inclusiveness inherent in inspiring commitment, meet the expectations people have of them to be more democratic and interpersonally oriented than men.[3,4] And as we well know, when they do not meet those expectations, they hazard being stuck behind that brick wall of "bitch."

In describing their dealings with nearly every aspect of management, successful women leaders say they are trying to make people feel a part of the organization. Women, more than men, are more likely to say that they strive to make people feel important and energized. And women encourage participation by including others in problem solving discussions rather than going through the analysis and reaching conclusions on their own.[5]

Type 3: Strategic Control

One female CEO admitted to having a hard time "letting go" of control. I thought, "Who doesn't?" When you consider that many men and women in the highest levels of leadership have built their reputation and personal brand on achieving stellar results, it's fairly easy to understand how difficult it is to entrust others to plan and execute an important initiative associated with them. And it is not just about getting the job done. Each leader has a signature way of doing and delivering, and it is difficult to give up control to someone who does things differently.

Strategic control is a way of steering—without micromanaging—critical initiatives that one has delegated or in which one has involved others. Executive women demonstrate this by focusing others on understanding and achieving exactly what they want to achieve and in the ways she wants to achieve it. It is a form of delegation, where the delegates feel they are leading the charge and that the executive is being collaborative in guiding them and watching their backs. Although there is an element of good project management, the key component of this competency is being able to articulate a vision and purpose so that designated agents can make decisions and act in accordance with how the leader would want them to act. It is a way of maintaining control and pushing an agenda while being collaborative. A woman who does not partner with her delegates and does not make them feel empowered will almost certainly be seen as a controlling "bitch."

In my consulting work, executive women from a variety of organizations have assessed themselves as being "less developed" in strategic control than the other competencies discussed in this book. Perhaps it is because this is a competency that requires perfecting the art of delegation, an ability that is difficult to develop for many professionals. The common sentiments "If you want it done right, you need to do it yourself" and "In the time it takes me to explain what I need, I could have done it already" are really expressions of discomfort with letting go of control. For women, though, it can also be that they don't know how to delegate without appearing bossy. Successful executive women have figured out how to delegate and let go of control—in a very controlled way. Little is left to chance.

One executive woman talked about a key business deal that she felt her "right-hand man" needed to drive in order to obtain developmental experience and visibility. But ultimately the success or failure of it was on her. She talked him through why the deal was critical to the organization, what the best result would be and how she would go about driving it. Then the control factor kicked in. "I said to him, 'I want to be briefed after the negotiating sessions, but just about the highlights. Let's assume that the day after each negotiating session you brief me by 10 a.m.'" The structure she placed on getting feedback from her delegate allowed

> *Successful executive women have figured out how to delegate and let go of control—in a very controlled way.*

her to make suggested course corrections along the way, so that she continued to maintain control. More importantly though, she finessed the situation so that her right-hand man felt that he was controlling the initiative and that she was working collaboratively with him so that they would both be successful.

Executive men generally do not relinquish control of critical initiatives. They exercise their power, and stay front and center. Of course successful executive men delegate and let others hold the reins from time to time, but when push comes to shove on a highly visible project, they tend to take control and assume the lead.

Len, the COO of an educational institution, in speaking of a new building initiative, said, "We had a couple of similar building projects and they were terrible, they were really terrible—bad architecture, bad presentation, bad everything. I felt that this one had to be great; I just sort of trusted my own judgment and no one else's, frankly. Maybe that sounds arrogant, but I really felt that way at the time, and I still do." Another man, in talking about an important initiative that he did not delegate, said, "I told them, 'This is my baby and I lent my name to it and created the vision for it.'"

Neither man suffered negative consequences from maintaining absolute control, and each brought their work to a successful conclusion. But a woman staunchly controlling the show, not *sharing* the management of an effort, would be seen as a self-aggrandizing bitch![6] Successful executive women get beyond this. They are masterful at maintaining control while still being seen as democratic and inclusive. And they are also masterful at giving up total control while creating conditions that make others perform well.

———

In all three forms of influence discussed in this chapter, women manage to wield power and do it in a collaborative and engaging way. They create emotional bonds with and among the people they lead. For successful women leaders, although persuasion, inspiring commitment, and strategic control are distinct competencies, the combination of the three create a whole greater than the sum of its parts. Because of this engaging, connecting way of leading people to a desired goal, executive women have a unique opportunity to be leaders and managers of change. Connecting to people, connecting others, collaboration, and inclusion offset the isolating feelings associated with breaking from what is known and venturing into the great unknown.

Successful women leaders can blend—first, the ability to win over others to their vision, showing them that they care about the same things; second, the ability to engage others and get their buy-in by soliciting their participation; and third, the talent to drive implementation through others by giving up control in a controlled way. By blending these competencies, they not only make others more comfortable with them taking the lead, they also make others more comfortable going through change. They can be seen as competent, in charge, and not labeled "bitch."

CHAPTER 6

Tell the Story: Conceptual Thinking

B y seeing trends in a sea of information and recognizing the relationships and connections among seemingly unrelated facts, successful executive women weave stories that explain the meaning of situations. They draw parallels between the situation at hand and past situations, sometimes using metaphors, to help others understand. And in sharing their insights in a simple straightforward way, they reduce or even eliminate the intimidation factor that comes with revealing brilliance. Successful women leaders don't flaunt their capability— not wanting to be behind the brick wall of "bitch," they package it as a helpful offering to their colleagues at all levels of the organization. Conceptual thinking is this ability to see patterns and piece together information, grasping and generating abstract concepts. It is thinking "big picture" and it is thinking creatively. It is having the imagination and insight to create something new and different.

Seeing Connections

A C-suite executive in a Fortune 50 company met with her CEO to suggest modifications to his timetable for a huge change initiative. She said:

> "We wanted to reduce our cost overhead structure vis-a-vis our sales. So I went to Jason and said, 'You may not realize that the data being gathered for the June report will have an impact on the material you are asking for in May. So either people are going to make the wrong decisions in May and then change them, or they're not going to meet your deadline; so I suggest you converge the two projects into one with a deadline in June.' He hadn't been aware of any relationship between the two projects, but when we talked it through he did."

Another executive woman said:

"I look at the business analysis and weave it together into a story, like 'Here's what happened here; here's what happened there,' I take those facts that may have been on different pages, in different reports; I take facts from other areas of the business, facts that people don't even put together; and I can say, 'Now these are the things that are critical.' I do that in a way that presents the whole picture as opposed to presenting a sequence of facts. You need the whole picture in order to decide what to do."

Research on the female mind shows that women can integrate myriad facts; they tend to gather more data that pertain to a topic than men do; and, they connect these details faster. In decision-making, women weigh more variables, consider more options and outcomes, and see more ways to proceed. It's called "web thinking."[1] Research actually shows that the bridge between hemispheres in the brain is thicker in women than in men, and the thicker connection allows for greater communication between the two hemispheres.[2] The right brain plays a larger role in interpreting nonverbal cues while interpretation of nonverbal data happens in the left cerebral cortex. The implication is that a greater left-right hemisphere connection makes it easier to assemble and integrate information. An October 2013 study published in the journal *Brain* reported that Einstein had more extensive connections between his two cerebral hemispheres than the average male brain and speculated that this may have been why he was a genius. By the way, there is no mention as to whether Einstein's brain was compared to the average female brain, but I digress.

The feminine propensity to look at business problems contextually, to concentrate on the whole of an issue rather than its parts[3], is a powerful capability and may tie back to the strong connection between the right and left hemispheres of the brain. So let's have a bit of fun with this! Perhaps this is the reason we hear the old adage that women have to work twice as hard and be twice as smart to get ahead.[4] If being smart is the proclivity for seeing connections, relationships and trends, women successfully climbing the ladder to leadership could indeed be "twice as smart"! And so as not to daunt their colleagues, women could indeed "work twice as hard" couching their smarts as "matter of fact" and "you can do this, too." Alice, the CEO of a multi-state non-profit organization, did exactly that when she presented an analysis to the mayor and his cabinet.

Alice recounted:

"I was co-architect with the mayor of a very big elaborate criminal justice plan. It was a huge analysis and very political. I was the budget point person so I had many opportunities to brief the mayor and come up with ideas. I remember going to a meeting to brief him about how police are deployed. I just briefly explained to him, 'This is the way this is, and this is what it means.' In front of his whole cabinet, he turned to everybody and said, 'Why can't you explain things the way she explains things?'"

Now mind you, the cabinet had not seen all the behind the scenes work she did gathering facts, making connections, mulling all of it over for multiple hours. It was rather like the cooking shows where they mix the ingredients, put the batter in a pan in the oven, and then magically pull out the finished cake. Alice was able to piece together an array of information and figure out what it meant behind the scenes, then effortlessly explain it to mayor and cabinet. Of course, to tamp down any intimidation caused by the suggestion that she was superior, she deflected the "Why can't you guys do this?" comment with a joke about her spending way too much time reading "whodunit" novels.

Sharing Your Thinking

A complementary skill to seeing connections and weaving everything into a coherent story is being able to tell that story in a way that makes one's audience feel smart *with* you, rather than feel intimidated *by* you. These women assume that you can keep up with them, and by doing so, it erases any air of superiority.

The CFO of a large pharmaceutical company told me, "Financial analysis is what I've been doing my whole life. I understand what it means, how to interpret it, how to use it." She's smart as a whip and figures that anyone can understand any concept if she explains it clearly enough. I felt this first hand, as a person with zero background in finance, when she explained a seemingly complicated issue around pension expense for her company and I got it!

Sharing your thinking in a non-intimidating way reflects a major theme that weaves through the whole Women's Leadership Blueprint—that is, switching the focus from "I" to "we," and being inclusive. Successful women can "bring you along," can speak intelligently so that you follow the reasoning and "connect the dots," rather than—and I despise this term but hear it all the time—"dumb it down" to make something understandable (to the lowly masses). As you can imagine, women perceived to be "smarter-than-thou," and placing themselves above their audience, sets up that brick wall of "bitch" to obstruct their path to leadership.

As discussed throughout this book, men have more latitude than women when it comes to displaying their expertise. This is not to say that men can't stray outside the bounds of acceptable by being overtly pompous and acting superior. The crux of the issue is that we readily accept men who are experts and are extremely capable; and unfortunately, we have a harder time accepting women with that capacity.

Another top executive, Donna, told me that she is a particularly good listener. She recalled:

> "We had an executive team meeting where I was presenting an analysis of our supply chain processes. I knew that this was a bit complex and might go over the heads of a few of my colleagues and I didn't want them to feel intimidated. When I got up from my seat, I said, 'As I walk through these findings, please stop me if you have any questions or concerns.' So about 10 minutes into my presentation, my colleague Sean did just that.

I did the active listening thing and repeated back to him what I heard him say. Then I said, 'I hear you, Sean. I was thinking the same thing at first.' And then I walked through my thought process."

Donna said she has made active listening a part of her personal brand because it is such a good way to stave off people's intimidation of her and her ability to think through complex issues.

Integrating Complex Information, Seeing Long-Term Implications

Lois, the EVP of human resources for a national store chain told me:

"I was talking with the CEO about 'when the economy comes back.' I thought, 'This whole thing is going to be different and we will need different people. The old way isn't going to be the way we are going to do it in the future.' So I said to him, 'We are going after a new market, and our touch points with customers will no longer be primarily with employees in our stores. We need people who can adapt to the new customer relationship; people who are a part of that new customer base.' I can synthesize things pretty well, look at things in different ways, from different angles, different perspectives and tell a story. The CEO knows I get the business piece and looks to me to translate it into the implications for our employees. He feels comfortable because I boil things down and don't go off into some complex theory."

Behind the scenes though, Lois did a lot of thinking and analysis to come up with her thesis. She looked at market trends, inside and outside her industry, and the emerging new economy and saw that there was no going "back to normal." The landscape had changed, and her company needed to anticipate the different future rather than seeing the bad economy as a temporary problem to ride out. She was focused on the longer-term strategy, not an immediate-term reaction. And she was able to deliver her reasoning and conclusions in a practical, conversational way.

Regina, a brilliant VP of operations at a giant consumer goods company, says that one of her primary functions is to translate operations to the rest of the organization. She told me, "If you are functionally right, but nobody understands it, you get no support." And she knew that this was particularly important when being "functionally right" meant a long-term strategy rather than a short-term fix.

She was faced with an issue of capacity constraint for the production of the company's number-one cookie brand and snack cracker line. Regina launched into her analysis:

> "When you look one layer below the surface, to look at capabilities of the line, what you find is that we have a tremendous amount of excess capability for products that aren't in demand or new products that we've launched and failed. We had 13 bakeries across the U.S. No bakery made all of our products; and no bakery was a sole source for any of our major products because of shipping cost and breakage issues. So we make our number one cookie in seven places all over the country."

Regina went on to explain how she looked at all the bakeries; whether they would save money by closing some of them; how many different oven lines were operating; and were they running flat out or idle some of the time.

She had come to the conclusion that there was not a capacity constraint when one took an enterprise-wide look, but in fact there was excess capacity. And closing a facility to consolidate would not save money; it would actually cost them more. Restructuring was the answer. She said, "I did the analysis, prepared a presentation, and explained it to everyone to get their buy-in; which I did." Regina was seen as a whiz kid, and her executive colleagues enjoyed her enthusiasm and delight in discovering the root of a problem and explaining it in simple terms. She was informative as well as entertaining. When she had the leadership team's buy-in, she involved multiple teams to figure out how to free up capacity for their big cookie brand and snack crackers.

In order to effectively make her case, Regina blended her skills to pull together facts, make sense of them, clearly explain her analysis and conclusions, and involve others in developing potential solutions. She took a holistic view of company operations—pulling together disparate information—in order to understand the capacity problem and ultimately design a sustainable fix (restructuring) rather than slapping on a Band-Aid for a short-term fix (buy another bakery). Engaging others in problem solving and execution played a vital role in her ability to make wide sweeping changes without people seeing her as a "bitch."

Seeing Parallels

Looking at two completely different issues, and seeing the synergy between the two, often leads to novel ideas. Executive women seem to be particularly talented in this. One executive I interviewed stands out in her ability to see parallels.

Sophie, the senior executive in an organization that provides training and employment told me about an "a-ha" moment she'd had:

> "I'm constantly focusing on the connection between drug treatment and employment. People are in prison on a drug offense, so everybody automatically assumes that drug treatment is the answer to their problems. Well, yes, but at the end of the day, they have to get jobs. What are drug treatment people doing about that? So I started thinking about the similarities between drug treatment and employment. There's the notion that relapse is an acceptable part of recovery. Everyone presumes that you might not make it the first time or the second time, and then I realized the same thing is true of employment. But most employment programs don't presume that. When someone doesn't make it on their first job, we just abandon them. You know, 'Well,

we tried. You screwed up. See ya.' I was thinking about that, and my 'a-ha' moment was when I figured out that we need to develop a program where when people fail, we have a mechanism for calling them back in, ask what happened, what can we do to make this better, and give them a second shot.' Just like you would if they relapsed on drugs. I'm able to pull those kinds of threads together, things that don't seem like they're connected into one coherent solution."

Conceptual thinking can be encouraged if it isn't spontaneous. In my company's work with clients we use a facilitation technique called an "excursion" to spur novel thinking and to prompt looking at an issue in a different way. People work on solving a "fun" problem then return to the problem they are facing and see what they can apply from the fun problem discussion.

A group of women insurance executives were discussing expanding their company's services into a new market. To help the creative juices flow we did an excursion: *Imagine that you are going to open a winery. What are the key steps? Who else will be involved? What services will be included? What resources will you need?* The executives broke up into smaller groups to discuss the scenario, and then returned to the large group to bring together all the ideas. Once those ideas were posted for all to see, we asked, "Okay. Let's find some ideas here that might work for you in expanding your insurance services into a new market." In doing this exercise, the executives were prompted to draw parallels between two unrelated situations, and novel, exciting ideas percolated in the discussion. It provided a platform where they could relax and have fun, taking them out of their real-life conundrum. There's nothing like tension to squash creativity, and nothing like removing tension to spark it!

Executive women employ conceptual thinking when they listen, watch, and investigate, integrating that information to understand the motives and values of others.

Executive women employ conceptual thinking when they listen, watch, and investigate, integrating that information to understand the motives and values of others. It is that understanding that provides them a platform to make the connection and have influence, as was discussed in an earlier chapter. Conceptual thinking is also the engine behind cultural and political awareness, another competency that is covered in the next chapter. By picking up on patterns and nuances, and piecing them together to create a clear picture of the environment, executive women sense the culture and the politics in an organization and adapt their behavior accordingly.

Women excel in being able to "translate" complex information into a story and to see trends. They see connections, draw parallels, and integrate complex information to help others in leadership make informed decisions. Importantly, they are able to share their insights in a clear, easy-to-understand narrative that keeps their audience from being "blown away," uncomfortable, or intimidated. After all, just as no one likes a "bitch," no one tolerates a "smarty pants" or, dare I say, a "smarty pantsuit."

CHAPTER 7

Navigate the Terrain: Cultural and Political Savvy

R eading the environment and using that awareness to tailor one's behavior is a powerful ability for leaders. Generally, successful women are particularly astute, grasping a culture or a group dynamic and figuring out how to best use that understanding to take effective action. This competency is an important application of conceptual thinking, because it requires a keen eye for picking up on patterns and nuances and piecing them together to create a clear picture of the environment. It also requires that one takes that picture and figures out how to navigate within it—in other words, how to use the picture as a tool to think through "If I do X, group A will do Y." At the basic level, believe it or not, successful navigation can start with wearing the right clothes!

One morning, at the office I worked in several years ago, I walked down the hall and saw a small group of my colleagues spontaneously gathered in the lobby area laughing and in a very animated discussion. One of the senior consultants, Bob, was looking very spiffy in a fashionable dress shirt and fun tie, an outfit that was a bit edgy and not his usual style. He had just returned from a meeting with a potential client looking rather pleased with himself. He said, "I went out last night shopping for something to wear to my meeting this morning." (He was meeting with executives from a clothing retailer that specializes in urban chic wear.) "I figured that if I want to get work with them, I should look like I speak their language."

The other guys were laughing, thinking it a bit ridiculous to go to an executive sales meeting without a traditional suit and tie. Bob thought that this was a brilliant idea, fitting into the client culture in order to win the account. I thought, "Wow—don't you do that all the time?"

But one shouldn't assume that "dressing the part" and working to fit in comes naturally to everyone. And believe it or not, that lack of awareness can mean the difference between success and failure. For example, Beverly, a senior principal of a global consulting firm, had a sales meeting with executives from Levi Strauss. It was a big deal; the project was huge and all the big consulting firms were vying for the work. Three other senior consultants from her firm joined her. Beverly and the three gentlemen arrived in town the night before the morning meeting and met for an early dinner. To her surprise, her colleagues were planning to wear suits and ties the next day. She said, "Here we are going to a company known for making jeans, and these guys will be in suits? No way!" She insisted that her colleagues go out and buy Dockers and polo shirts to wear to the meeting. The next day, the team assembled in their casual finery. When they arrived for the meeting, they watched the parade of men in well-tailored-suits saunter in and out of the conference room. The guys were squirming, feeling uncomfortable that they were not in their suits like the competition but Beverly remained confident in her approach. After the meeting, the men were convinced that they had blown it. They didn't show the professional polish that the other firms had. What happened? Two days later, Beverly got the call that they had, in fact, been selected. She recalled, "They said that our proposal was similar to the other firms, but the thing that really differentiated us was that we 'got their culture.'"

Organizational culture is a set of behavioral norms and values; it's "the way work gets done here."[1] It's a nonverbal communication that is interactive. Just as the "listener" has an active role in influencing the speaker[2], culture plays an active role in influencing behavior—if you are paying attention. That means that you are aware of the cues and nuances imbedded in the physical environment: how people interact, who interacts, when they interact, who speaks and who does not, how people dress (Bob got that one), what pictures are on the wall. With some companies, such as Levi Strauss, the culture is evident from their brand.

Why is it that men seem not to be as good as women at sensing culture and it's importance? Some of it may be brain chemistry. Helen Fisher, biological anthropology professor at Rutgers, talks about innate tendencies and proclivities "built into the architecture of the gendered brain millennia ago.[3] Among the list of characteristics baked into the female brain are: a capacity to read postures, gestures, facial, expressions and nonverbal cues; emotional sensitivity; empathy; a broad contextual view of any issue; and a preference for cooperating. Sounds like the kind of mental tools one needs to be culturally sensitive! Men, on the other hand, have innate abilities that include a superb understanding of spatial relations, an ability to solve complex mechanical problems, an ability to focus their attention, and an ability to control many of their emotions. These skills are important in other ways, but they aren't very helpful in reading culture.

Cultural savvy is a competency that women most likely develop from a very early age. Women are "used to" adapting to the environment or culture, because they have been socialized to do so and have had to do so in order to fit in and be successful. So in addition to brain chemistry, there is social reinforcement that hones women's ability to read culture.

My friend Linda's 9-year-old daughter came home from her first day in a new school, announcing that she "needed" to learn how to make people laugh! She said that during Morning Meeting the kids take turns answering a fun question, so she wanted to practice being funny like her new classmates were that day. She rehearsed with her mom to come up with amusing answers to questions. Her daughter then felt prepared to truly be a part of the class's culture. She picked up on the

Cultural savvy is a competency that women most likely develop from a very early age. Women are "used to" adapting to the environment or culture, because they have been socialized to do so and have had to do so in order to fit in and be successful.

dynamics of her new school right away and worked to become a part of it. On the other hand, Linda's 11-year-old son, when asked what the new school was like, shrugged and said, "The classrooms are bigger and there are more windows."

In Deborah Tannen's work on cross-gender communication, she found that women adapt their style to the environment. For instance, women communicate differently in a mixed group than they do in a group of just women. Men, however, communicate in the same way whether they are with just men or with both men and women.

Men haven't had the same pressure as women to consider the culture and adapt accordingly. Those who are in the majority seldom do. After all, the upper echelon of the corporate world has historically had a male-influenced culture; it's not foreign to men; there's no need to adapt to it, and they don't even think about it, unless it is staring them in the face. An executive woman from a very large software company was in Asia for a business meeting followed by a reception that she described as a big party with a cover band. She said, "I leave the bar to go down to the restroom. There's always a line for the women's bathroom, right? There are 40 men in line, all these executives and sales guys, and there's not one woman in line! " Then she joked,

"Nothing like a line for the restroom to make the point about who dominates the executive culture!" Perhaps that lack of pressure to adapt to business, and to other male-dominated spheres of society, leave men a bit flat-footed when it comes to reading the nuances of organizational culture.

But women do have to adapt. In a McKinsey report about gender diversity in top management[4], close to 40 percent of female respondents in their survey of 1,400 managers and executives indicated that women's leadership and communication styles are incompatible with the prevailing styles in the top management of their companies. In the simplest of terms, one executive woman told me, "When I'm talking to my male colleagues, I deepen my voice, I speak more slowly and not as bubbly. And I'm very precise and to the point when I speak or when I e-mail." This adaptation goes right back to proactively managing colleagues' perceptions to avoid negative stereotypes—in this case, battling the gendered stereotype of being "ditzy" or "flighty." A woman who is "bubbly" runs the hazard of being seen as unintelligent. A woman who has a voice that is more soprano than alto risks being seen as a lightweight. So women leaders have to be concerned about not only being labeled a "bitch," but also with being labeled a ditz if they do not adapt to the male culture.

For women, being astute is a ticket to entry to the highest levels of business. Cultural savvy was demonstrated when the head of sales and marketing for a large global company engineered a strategy for changing the way the firm interacts with clients before and after a sale. She said, "The salespeople are used to being in front of the customer; we had to teach them different ways to present, because the way you present in person is different than the way you present virtually." She set up a virtual studio and arranged training for the sales reps. She told me, "We taught them how to do it, and now there are contests around the globe on who can do this the best. Every quarter we recognize a region; the leadership teams are incentivized, the market units are incentivized; the people on the ground are incentivized. All you have to do around here is stage a contest; competition is just a part of the culture so I leveraged that."

One executive woman described her company's culture this way: "It's always a fast-moving, high-paced environment. It's not an environment in which one could sit around with people and say, 'What do you think? What if we did this, or what about that?' You can do that one-on-one, but not in a formal meeting." In her company, the culture didn't accommodate brainstorming. She knew that testing ideas required putting forward a proposal and rationale after gathering input informally.

Another woman in the C-suite of a Fortune 100 company said the culture of her company was different than others where she had worked. She came from a company that had an in-your-face, cutthroat culture where people challenged each other, often using "colorful" language. Now she was in a culture that was conservative and "polite." She said:

> "In one of my first staff meetings I said, 'Did anybody see the sitcom with Tim McGraw last night?' One of the people that worked for me said, 'Yeah, and the very first word he said was a curse word.' And I said, 'Really? What did he say?' He said, '"Damn.' I thought, 'Oh, that's a curse word? I'm in trouble.' But I held my tongue and decided I had to clean up my language."

She also noticed right away how "nice" people were and very willing to collaborate with one another. She said, "After dealing with the back biting and competitiveness in my previous company, it was an absolute pleasure to work in this culture." And she happily adapted very quickly.

Sandra, an SVP, told me, "I had a difficult situation come up in my first year with the company where a key deliverable for the CEO, that was a responsibility I shared with one of my peers, James, had slipped through the cracks. I had completed what I was supposed to do, but he did not." She said:

> "If I was still at my former company, I would have documented it with CYA memos to head-off any backstabbing. But here, and I much prefer this, I can just go talk to people and work it out. I went to James's office and sat down and said, 'Okay, let's figure out a resolution.' I realized early on that this culture is collaborative and no one points fingers. I know that sounds too good to be true, but that's the way you have to play here."

Cultural Savvy vs. Political Savvy

Political and cultural savvy are quite similar. Just as with cultural savvy, political savvy requires one to pay attention to cues and behave accordingly. However, with political savvy, as we have traditionally defined it, the focus is on power, or "who's who at the zoo." It's more about the personal dynamics within the organizational dynamics.

As discussed previously, women show strength in cultural savvy and men show less. Not so with political savvy. This is a behavioral competency where men appear to show strength, demonstrating it twice as much as executive women. Furthermore, women rate the competency among the least important, whereas men rate it among the most important!

Why is that? Research indicates that although executive women are astute observers of their corporate cultures, they claim that "knowledge of corporate politics" has nothing to do with their success.[5] This is consistent with my own research findings.

Research indicates that although executive women are astute observers of their corporate cultures, they claim that "knowledge of corporate politics" has nothing to do with their success.

Charting the Political Environment

Women do not demonstrate Political Savvy as readily as men, and there is a difference in *how* it is demonstrated. For men, political savvy is about navigating power and hierarchy in order to advance or maintain their status. For women, political savvy is more about reading and understanding the power dynamics among individuals and groups in order to work with them and fit in.

Political savvy was evident when Kelli, a Fortune 100 SVP, agreed to lead phase two of a companywide re-engineering project, implementing cost-saving measures that would potentially cut back on facilities. It was her job to validate and break out by function the savings that had been identified in phase one. At first she didn't want to take it on. She said to the CFO, "We can call this reengineering; we can call it whatever we'd like, but this is a productivity program, so everybody is going to hate the person who leads this effort." The political climate was a real problem. There were pockets in the organization where key stakeholders had not been involved up-front in the project. She noted, "I knew that there might be some big minefields. So we literally met with every single team; we validated and probed." Kelli, along with her finance guy and systems guy, engaged every functional team in reviewing what phase one identified as cost savings. She and the teams looked at the investment required to realize those savings to understand the real benefit to the company, if any. They also explored any new ideas for cost savings. She managed to navigate the political minefields and to get the cooperation of people across the company. Not only that, but this approach gave her the knowledge she needed to present the executive leadership team with well-supported recommendations for reengineering all aspects of product production.

Political Savvy demonstrated by men tends to be about being able to interpret the underlying reasons for power shifts and using that understanding to protect or increase their own power. Len, a Fortune 100 COO, who was one of two potential heirs-apparent to the CEO, knew that his difficult relationship with a peer had political roots. He said, "I was being used as a foil to pry him along so I was really an antagonist to him and that's a natural human thing, you know. I was a big pain in the butt to him and every time he did something wrong I think they would hold up a picture of me and say, 'Hey, he's ready,' you know, 'in case you don't do better.'" Len knew that his peer would not go out of his way to help him. In fact, he was someone he couldn't readily trust, and Len felt he had to watch his back.

Another COO, Jeff, described why a group of people in his organization suddenly shifted their attitude about supporting their food services workers after the decision (his) had been made to outsource. He explained:

"They rallied around the issue of 'these poor wonderful people' who had been doing this work all these years. A week before, if I had asked them about Joe Smith managing the deli counter, they would have said, 'I hate that SOB. He's the worst provider I've ever seen.' But now Joe becomes the victim of outsourcing. That's what really turned their attitude. People looked at this and said, 'Wow. Nothing like this has ever happened here. We don't like it. We've got to stop it.' I was able to weather that storm and stand my ground. I reiterated how much better services will be and that the new workers would become a part of our community."

Both Jeff and Len used their understanding of power dynamics to avoid being undercut by potential threats to their authority or status.

For women, political savvy is also about being able to analyze the political dynamics of a situation—but rather than using it to gain a power advantage, they use it to operate effectively within the situation. One female CEO, Michelle, deliberately created a meeting dynamic that would be to her benefit by adding another person to the meeting. She said of the person she was meeting with, "He was a very difficult person to manage, just volatile. I had a hard time telling him what I meant. I asked the CFO to participate in that meeting. He's a friend of mine. He really knows me. I knew he would help me." Michelle engineered a situation where she could be effective, and she knew that her friend the CFO would figure out why he was there and what role he should play. Apparently, the CFO was also rather politically savvy.

Sharon, a CHRO in the chemical industry, works as a partner to her colleagues to describe the dynamics in the organization. She illuminates for them issues about where people are aligned, where there are the pockets of resistance, where there are tensions, and why. But sometimes she acts as a translator of group processes for members of the executive team. The CEO actually said to her, "I don't usually have a clue what's going on in a group. I know the content, the facts, but I don't know whether there are issues in the room or in the organization at large." Sharon was valued for her ability to anticipate reactions and help her male colleagues see obstacles and mitigate them. Although these men may be politically savvy in ways that maintain or advance them in the pecking order, reading the bigger picture of group dynamics where their hierarchical status isn't affected is not part of it. But for Sharon and Michelle, seeing and navigating the group dynamics are what political savvy is all about.

Not "Playing Politics"

Perhaps women downplay the importance of political savvy because they view it as "playing politics" and therefore distasteful. I've heard this many times from women leaders. It gets back to politics being about power and hierarchy. And women don't "play" that way; I dare say this goes all the way back, once again, to when we were children.

All boy groups and all girl groups develop different styles for interacting. Boys and girls play games that support development of different competencies.[6]

Boys learn about competition and develop skills for resolving conflict. Their games require coordinating activity, supporting development of organizational and leadership skills. They learn how to gain and maintain status in the male hierarchy. So as boys grow up they see the world in terms of their place in a hierarchical social order where they are either "one-up" or "one-down." I saw this first hand when my son, who was 5 years old at the time, was dismayed that my business partner and I had the same title, being co-owners of our company. He asked, "But Mom, who is *really* the boss?" (He wanted very much for me to be "one-up.") When boys negotiate, it is about trying to achieve or maintain the upper hand and to protect themselves from others' attempts to put them down.[7]

Perhaps women downplay the importance of political savvy because they view it as "playing politics" and therefore distasteful.

Girls, on the other hand, play games that emphasize the importance of cooperation and the development of noncompetitive skills. Games like house and dolls are role-playing games that are not about competition. Girls grow up seeing the world in terms of being an individual in a network of connections. Negotiation is to resolve conflict, to gain support, to close a rift, to be closer, and to gain consensus. Although there are hierarchies in their world, girls' hierarchies are of friendship rather than of power and accomplishment.[8]

A work colleague of mine, a professor at the University of Minnesota, taught a business management class where his students researched the most important issues that derailed women in their professional advancement. One of the top issues they identified was that women did not know how to compete and be a team member at the same time. They attributed this to women not having been as involved in team sports as men were. This graduate research was conducted more than 30 years ago. What struck me about this is that women are more involved in team sports now than they were 30 years ago, but in my work with emerging leaders, it is clear to me that women are still struggling to blend competing and collaborating!

In the very first pages of *The Confidence Code*[9], Katty Kay and Claire Shipman convey their experience observing and talking with two women who play professional basketball. On the court, the women "had an air of command" about them; off court, they expressed something very different, as did some of the coaches. One woman said, (bolded words are my emphasis) "Let's say I had a bad game. I'll think, 'Oh **we** lost' and I'll feel like I wanted to **help the team** win and win **for the fans**.' With guys, they think 'I had a bad game' and shrug it off." Another woman said that the women don't get aggressive with one another because women **get hurt feelings**, but guys just curse each other out and then forget about it. The authors point out that the women made the comparison between themselves and men with every comment.

Clearly they saw the contrast between how men are team players and how women are team players. What I also noticed in the responses from these female basketball players was that they appeared to be more focused on the collaborating, on the "doing for others," and not so much on the competing. And, they clearly drew a contrast between their experience and men's experience. So much for pushing team sports as a way to prepare young women for competing to advance professionally while also being a "team player."

So getting back to "playing politics," it's no small wonder that women find it distasteful. Politics is about power and about winning power, and, for women, that isn't a team sport. As girls, maintaining relationships was more important than winning and proving superiority. But also, it seems that women see competition (for power) and collaboration (to maintain relationships) as characteristics that don't mix.

Professional services firms, structured as partnerships, also abhor political behavior. Researchers found that senior executives from multiple global firms avoided the words *power* and *politics*, although these firms are rife with politics.[10] Such concepts to these executives seem suspect and threatening to their sense of collegiality within the partnership. It would appear that in a culture that depends highly on a shared leadership model and sense of collegiality, both men and women eschew politics and power, seeing them as damaging to collaboration.

I asked an executive woman, who told me she does not play politics, to tell me what playing politics meant to her. She was immediately and profusely fluent! First (without prompting) she drew a distinction between playing politics and political savvy. She said, "I think I am politically savvy, meaning I understand how companies work, and how they make decisions, and I understand who the key stakeholders are to get things approved and done."

When she came to explaining playing politics, she spoke about it with contempt, as if it was the most despicable thing someone could do in an organization. She said, "Playing politics is undercutting others, not being direct and just saying the 'right things' or playing it safe and backstabbing where it suits yourself. You put yourself before the company and what is right." In other words, it is about being self-centered and gaining advantage over others—winning power. But to her, it also meant hurting others to get ahead.

There is another angle here about why successful women distance themselves from playing politics, and again it goes back to the fact that politics is about power. They know that if they are seen as powerful, it might not be such a good thing. As discussed in the first chapter on stereotypes, there is "fear of Lilith," a subconscious per-ceived threat associated with women wielding power that takes a lot of work to overcome. The successful women leaders do overcome it, by "sharing the power." Playing politics—or using political savvy to build power—puts women behind that brick wall labeled "bitch."

The way executive women use political savvy has all the markings of modifying the typical male behavior—that is, they strip out the hierarchical power aspects of it. And given the issues discussed so far, you can understand why. The competency, as women demonstrate it, is more about understanding the culture and dynamics in order to work within them effectively than it is about navigat-ing the power dynamics in order to advance or maintain their hierarchical status.

CHAPTER 8

Make Them Comfortable: Tempering Assertiveness

B y virtue of their gender, and the stereotypes that inadvertently leap to mind, we expect female authority figures to be engaging, comforting, and encouraging—and if we don't get clear signals that they meet these expectations, we can see them as threatening and, yes, label them a "bitch." Successful women in business are driven yet humorous, warm, or calming, thereby toning down their assertiveness. They break down tension and put others at ease without diminishing their status of authority. As discussed in earlier chapters, executive women temper assertiveness by toning down how they demonstrate confidence, the drive to achieve, and the power of influence. But in addition to filing down the sharp edges of those competencies they develop a personal brand that garners respect and creates a personal aura of relatability and approachability that broadly tempers all aspects of their leadership. Executive women achieve this relatability and approachability in a variety of ways, as each has her own personal style.

Sharing a Laugh

Ellen, the CEO of a large nonprofit, walks out on stage at a conference to present the results of a novel controversial social program to a national audience of 400 executive directors of other agencies and public policy officials. The room feels tense. Ellen comes center stage in front of the podium, followed by her COO and CFO. She looks at the audience and says, "Okay, let me just hit this head-on." She pauses for effect. "I am 5 foot 1." She pauses and dramatically tilts her head up, looking at the guys on either side of her; the audience laughs. "Steve is six four and John is six five. So just get over it." More laughter from the audience. "I've worked in a lot of organizations and I still can't manage to get a job where I don't hear, 'Here comes Mutt and Jeff.' Why do I keep doing this to myself?" The audience added applause to their laughter.

Ellen told me, "If you ask me what is the single thing that has helped me most in my professional life, I would not hesitate to say it's my sense of humor. There is no question about it; it transcends everything. It transcends ethnic barriers, class barriers, gender barriers. It's my prize possession. It has helped me enormously in terms of how I relate to men, how I participate in a man's world." She continued, "I have gone out of my way to soft pedal how assertive and on the ball I am because I'm afraid people will go 'Whoa!' and back away. My humor defuses situations so I don't come off as obnoxious and know-it-all-ish."

Abby, a C-suite executive of a Fortune 500 company, uses her Southern accent as a convenient target of her self-deprecating humor. It was a particularly effective vehicle when Tennessee-based Oak Ridge National Laboratories caught heat in the news for announcing that it was going to offer a six-week "Southern accent reduction" course to their employees. Abby said, "We had a board call, and I was talking through something, and one of the board members said, 'Did you say this?' I said, 'No, I said something else,' then I said, 'Apparently I need to go through that Southern accent reduction course at Oak Ridge!' Everyone just cracked up."

On Mahogany Row the executive floor of a high-tech company, the stellar head of global executive compensation, Colleen, stepped just out of her office doorway to greet a senior analyst in her group who had come upstairs to give her an expedited report. In her shirtsleeves, suit jacket still draped on the back of her desk chair, Colleen struck a jaunty pose with an eager smile. After she said, "Hey, Sue. Whatcha got for me?" Colleen glanced down at a salad dressing stain on her suit skirt, rolled her eyes, and said, "You'd think with all the lunches I eat at my desk, I might think to use a napkin," then guffawed, looking at Sue, and said, "Right? Like, how dumb is that!" Colleen instantly dissolved Sue's tension of being on Mahogany Row and handing over her work that would soon be scrutinized. Sue played along saying, "Well, Colleen, next time I'll bring up some napkins!" Colleen's executive assistant jumped into the mix, grinning and saying, "Great. Make sure they are the *big* ones." Colleen's self-deprecating humor goes from cubicle to boardroom, and despite her assertive, confident aura, she instantly endears herself to people at all levels of her company.

Self-deprecating humor has long been a mainstay of executives wanting to project humbleness.

Self-deprecating humor has long been a mainstay of executives wanting to project humbleness. Some use it for effect, but it isn't authentic. For some leaders, though, it is a natural part of who they are. It is a quality that makes *them* comfortable, not wanting to appear pompous or superior, and thereby makes their audience comfortable. If it is genuine, it can be an essential tool for women leaders to effectively temper assertiveness and ward off that "bitch" label. The success of a male leader is not as contingent on tempering assertiveness, and, from what I have seen, men use humor quite differently. Whereas women use their humor to disarm people, men use humor to subtly give negative feedback or to knock someone down a peg who is trying to take a dominant position over them.

As discussed in earlier chapters, men can get away with displaying their mastery far more than women can. Of course, women have to strike the right balance between being seen as the expert and being self-deprecating to the extent that they "put themselves down." One of the common ways of doing that is aiming self-deprecating humor at personal characteristics or habits, such as Ellen's height, Abby's Southern accent, and Colleen's absence of a lunch napkin, not at their capability and expertise.

Of course, humor isn't always self-deprecating. One executive woman told me, "I was always called 'bossy' as a kid. But, I *was*. I have four brothers, I had to be." So I asked, "How can you be bossy and still be so well liked as a leader?" She said, "It's a style thing. You do it with a smile; you do it with a joke. It's not so hard. I think it goes to emotional intelligence. It is knowing how you're coming across to people."

Another executive women said, "I've always had male friends; I am just comfortable with men. In meetings where someone is trying to give me a hard time, I've said, 'Hey, I have brothers, okay. If you're going to go down that road, you're going to have to try a lot harder than that!'" She is kidding around to share a laugh, but underlying it she is also letting her male colleagues know that she can be one of the guys, she knows the ropes in the male world, and that they can be comfortable and be themselves with her. And of course, she is also letting them know that they can't get away with anything.

Showing Empathy

Many of us have tried very hard to contain our emotions as professionals, because in the work environment, traditionally shaped by a male culture, being emotional is not valued and is seen as unprofessional.

What makes this issue of emotions at work so loaded is that it is very gendered. Emotions are associated with women, particularly the emotions expressed with tears. I was a facilitator at a leadership development conference for top tier leaders at a financial company where we focused on the characteristics that the company wanted to develop in future leaders. After finishing my part of the agenda, another facilitator came to the front of the room to talk about giving performance feedback. He said, "I know you *guys* find this difficult (there were both women and men in the audience)—having to give feedback to someone. I know what it's like. You give a performance review to a secretary. In the middle of your feedback (his eyes rolling like everyone knew what was coming next) I'm getting out the tissue box." He then mimicked crying, wiping his eyes and talking with a high voice. "You know how women get, crying at this stuff." I about died on the spot, watching this in the back of the room. I scanned the audience of 50 people, eight of whom were women, to gauge their reactions, sure that I was going to have to do damage control because of this insanely awful bozo at the front of the room. Sadly it was only me and the other women in the room who were insulted by Mr. Bozo's performance.

I frequently see groups of people take the Myers-Briggs, and women often lament when they come out an "F" indicating a preference for using their feelings when decision-making, versus a "T" indicating a prefer-ence for using a thought process to do so. Using feelings suggests to them that they are not being logical and pro-fessional. They know those who are emotional at work are viewed disparagingly. It's a bit of a double bind for women when you think that being emotional is mushy and unprofessional, while being unemotional and professional is bitchy. Of course, those perceptions don't come out of nowhere. Corporate work cultures still discourage us from using our feelings as legitimate data to help analyze a situation, to help make decisions, and to help us be effective. "Fact-based decision-making," by which they mean "void of emotion," is still a mantra for executive teams as they grapple with issues and how to solve them.

Corporate work cultures still discourage us from using our feelings as legitimate data to help analyze a situation, to help make decisions, and to help us be effective.

But there is a wide variety of "being emotional," and whereas one side of the scale is not professional (angry outbursts, crying jags), the other side (empathy) is another useful tool in the getting-beyond-"bitch" toolbox.

One CEO told me, "By being willing to let my emotional side show and having empathy for someone when they've made a mistake, I'm able to say, 'How can we help them get over that? Can we shore them up?'" Her empathy for others was evident in how she engaged her executive team, her staff, and her company's external partners. She truly sought to understand how a person or group was feeling, acknowledge those feelings and demonstratively relate to them, all the while conducting business, holding people accountable for their results, and asking them to take on more or to do better. She chalked it up to "just being herself." Her colleagues did not see her as being soft or "mushy."

Kathy, the CEO of a health science company, told me about an important high-powered business negotiation she'd recently conducted:

> "One day we had some guests in for a major business deal we were considering. It was a hot day, so I ran down to the soda machines and got some sodas for them. I remember Gary, our COO saying, 'This wouldn't happen anywhere else, the boss getting the drinks.' I thought, 'Why stand on ceremony? Why shouldn't I offer them something to drink?!' You have to recognize people's needs and be sensitive to them."

Kathy is a smart, tough leader, and there she was treating her visiting colleagues like guests in her home. Her graciousness and empathy for her "guests" offset her aggressiveness and intensity of purpose in the negotiation, and she succeeded in striking the deal she wanted.

Melissa, an executive of a Southeastern utility, dealt with two hurricanes in 10 months, one of which caused its 750,000 metered customers to lose power. She said:

"It was devastating. There was flooding; about 14 people died in the area. Forty of us were in the storm center that was built to withstand Level 5 hurricanes. Well some of the hurricane shutters failed at 1:30 a.m. when the eye of the hurricane came through our region. Our logistics head was in the room getting ready for the next day when we would have to get the power back on and a plate glass window fell on him. He had glass all over him when he crawled out of the room. I was picking glass out of his forehead and back. It was pretty much of a panic. I knew that it was a real test of leadership; I was calm and so others calmed down. We got through the night. The storm goes through. We get up the next morning and there's devastation everywhere. So I got our team together and said, 'Our job is not to bring power back; our job is to bring hope back to this community that things can get back to normal. Because until you have electricity, things can't get back to normal. People are depending on us to get

their lives back. Yeah, things are bad, but we're going to get through this and it's going to be better."

Melissa's empathy for her staff at the storm center, and for their customers, engendered trust that pulled them together to cope with the terrible circumstances.

Another executive woman, Alice, who "flies around the planet" to keep tabs on her leaders' progress and to problem solve with them said, "I'm the big boss arriving on the scene so people will naturally feel a bit uptight. I am direct but I massage it so they don't clam up. It's really about having strong emotional intelligence." She continued, "I watch my male colleagues in the same meeting that I'm in and they aren't doing what I'm doing. They aren't doing the endearment thing, but I do that because I want people to be at ease." She thinks men with the big title and big job want to be more intimidating and show their power. "For me it's not about power; it's about respect," she said. Alice finds that she gets more respect when she empathizes with the people reporting to her. However, she made it clear that she still holds people accountable. She recalled, "I went to India and they really screwed something up, and I'm like, 'Really? What's your plan to fix this? I want to see it and we're going to have the follow-up conversation here.' But I also acknowledged their embarrassment and regret that they'd not gotten the job done. I wanted them to know that I understood how they felt."

Whereas cultural savvy, another getting-beyond-"bitch" behavior we discussed earlier, is about being tuned in to the norms of the environment, empathy is being tuned in to the emotions of the individual. It is externally focused. Angry outbursts or tears of frustration are self-focused. The former is a productive, socially aware ability, whereas the latter is only productive in the sense that it is a personal release of tension. Women, more than men, excel at being able to feel what others are feeling, not surprising given how we are brought up and socialized.

The movement in corporate America to embrace the principles of Dan Goleman's "Emotional Intelligence" leadership model has brought awareness that emotions can be a valuable asset at work—for everyone.

The movement in corporate America to embrace the principles of Dan Goleman's "Emotional Intelligence" leadership model has brought awareness that emotions can be a valuable asset at work—for everyone.[1] Successful women leaders are ahead of men in this regard because they have learned to use their emotional intelligence to temper assertiveness, and make others feels comfortable, so that they can be a demanding leader without being labeled a—well, you know.

Establish Common Ground

One CEO said that as she moved up the corporate ladder, she had developed a "keen interest in sports." And she displayed it prominently in her office with a signed photograph of Roger Federer on the wall and strategically placed New York Mets paraphernalia. Sports as a great unifier may seem superficial, and it is a quintessential element of the stereotypical male work culture, but it can serve the purpose of a "universal connector." Hierarchical differences melt away in the face of bonding over a shared interest, and thus tempers assertiveness.

In the formality of the workplace where people tend not to talk about personal details, the topic of sports is a non-personal vehicle for connecting with others and is an easy platform to engage in conversation. But sports aren't the only common ground. The photos, artwork, or other paraphernalia that decorate the offices of men and women at all levels of an organization can serve as a platform for connecting. But when it is an executive, those everyday items have the power to shade hierarchical differences, and for women, as discussed so many times in these pages, that is more critical than it is for men. It gets back to women creating a personal aura of relatability and approachability that tempers assertiveness.

One executive said that she establishes common ground by keeping a running joke going when she's in a tough meeting. This technique is actually quite clever when you look at group dynamics. An essential of bringing together a group is to have a shared set of goals, but it goes beyond that. As groups become more cohesive they tend to differentiate themselves as a unique entity, separate from the rest of their surroundings. Work teams will kid about getting jackets, coming up with a cool name, having a secret handshake, all of which says we are insiders and have a shared understanding that others outside the group don't have. So creating that sense of "group-ness" is quite an effective way of tamping down discomfort and hierarchy. So keeping a running joke going in a meeting isn't being the class clown, again, it's about reinforcing the group and providing "comic relief" as they plow through tense discussions.

Of course the ultimate goal in establishing common ground and interests is building relationships. Developing relationships takes time, whereas establishing common ground creates immediate rapport.

All of the various ways of tempering assertiveness are equal-opportunity vehicles—that is, they are beneficial for both women and men in leadership roles. My research shows that executive women display evidence of this competency more frequently than men, and, because of women's propensity to be empathetic, they demonstrate it in more ways than men. This is evidence that women feel it is more crucial for their effectiveness and success.

Developing relationships takes time, whereas establishing common ground creates immediate rapport.

Successful women leaders have found their own authentic way to break down tension and put others at ease without diminishing their status of authority. Whether through humor, empathy, or common ground, they breakdown hierarchical barriers—and of course break through the "bitch" wall—to lead assertively in a collaborative, inclusive way. As one executive woman put it, "I consider myself first among equals."

CHAPTER 9

Plan Your Route: Self-Development Savvy

As we all know from countless books, headlines, and our own personal experiences, men advance their careers higher and faster than women. Successful executive men get "pulled up" by other men at higher levels of their organization far more than women. Some women do get to the top. They just take self-directed nontraditional routes.

Women take charge of their careers, ensuring that they are getting the experiences they need in order to attain top leadership. They are proactive about managing their progression: watching for "path pavers," the positions that are steppingstones to their goal and people who will help them, and "advancement derailers," the positions that might sound good but lead nowhere.

Successful executive men get "pulled up" by other men at higher levels of their organization far more than women. Some women do get to the top. They just take self-directed nontraditional routes.

Self-development savvy is a competency that successful women use to bolster the relatively little support and advocacy they get from top executives. Instead of complaining (some call it "whining") or being angry and bitter (getting behind that brick wall of "bitch") about organizational barriers, successful executive women take positive action by figuring out what jobs and people will pave their way to the top, and stepping onto those routes.

Rita, the CEO of a utility, said she had been passed over for a promotion earlier in her career. Her manager gave her average performance ratings and was deliberately holding her back. She said:

"You can either get bitter and blame the company, or you can realize this is this guy's fault and he's not gonna change your hard work. I chose the latter and it made all the difference. Within two years, his supervisor was changed out. The new guy knew my work; so I went to him and said, 'There's a job opening I want to bid on.' It was a large step up; but I knew it would position me for more advancement and I knew I could get his support."

Marion, the CEO of a life sciences organization, told me, "I realized if I was ever going to run a business for the company, I'd better get some sales experience, so I asked to be transferred to that department." Once she had that experience as a sales manager, she took a job as planning manager for pharmaceuticals, where she interfaced between the VP of the division and the plants, making sure operations had the resources and budget needed to implement the division's strategic plan. "I got exposure to the management committee and got to see things at a more strategic level," she said. She went on to take a district sales manager role because it was "one of the defining jobs in pharmaceuticals" then became a plant manager because "it will give me the experience I need to run one of the company's businesses." Marion knew her company's businesses well and took advantage of its informal routes of advancement.

Executive men that I have interviewed don't talk about how they worked to gain broad experience that would prepare them for their upper management role; women do. Men don't talk about how they made sure they did a stint in sales or marketing or research because that was the functional area that was the proving ground for up and coming executives; women do. Marion said:

> "I saw younger guys hop through a lot fewer jobs than I did, and they had to demonstrate a lot less than I did. They came up the ladder faster, in much more of a "stovepipe"-type career that didn't have as broad an experience base. It took me more plodding and stepwise progression, whereas they were able to take the stairs two at a time. But I'm better off for it, with the broader skill set, I turned out to be a hell of a lot better."

A successful woman's career path can often be described as taking the scenic route, not necessarily following the straight, more direct line, or climbing the corporate ladder one step at the time.[1] Women take *more* steps and *more* jobs—sideways and upward—to get to top leadership roles. A *Harvard Business Review* study in November 2014 reported that for the 24 women who are CEOs of Fortune 500 companies, their median stint at the same company before assuming the CEO role was 23 years. For a similar sample of male CEOs, it was 15 years.[2] Very capable women often get stuck in place, waiting longer than men to be promoted to the next level. By taking side steps within the organization, they can increase their knowledge and visibility, and their chances of being recognized and finally getting that promotion. Researchers Alice Eagly and Linda Carli say that women must navigate through the labyrinth, overcoming barriers and dead ends along the way to leadership roles.[3] Though men advance their careers higher and at faster rates than women[4], as Marion points out, the richness of her broad experience made her a better chief executive because it showed her all the ins and outs of the business and connected her with a cross-functional selection of people.

Women take more steps and more jobs— sideways and upward—to get to top leadership roles.

Mary Barra, CEO of General Motors, is another example of an executive woman who built broad experience on her 30-year path to the corner office. After starting her career as a senior engineer at a Pontiac plant, she got her MBA and took the job of manager of manufacturing planning. She went on to the take the executive assistant role to GM's CEO and the vice chairman, a position that would gain her broad exposure to the business globally. Three years later, Ms. Barra moved into the position of general director of communications, and then was an executive director of competitive operations engineering before taking a plant manager job at an assembly plant. Her next job was as vice president of global manufacturing engineering, followed by executive director of vehicle manufacturing engineering. (Whew—are we there yet?) Next, Ms. Barra served as vice president of global human resources, and two years later she took the role of senior vice president of global product development for two and a half years. She served as executive vice president of global product development and global purchasing and supply chain for five months, and *then* Ms. Barra was named chief executive officer.

Beginning with their first positions, women are often excluded from certain roles deemed critical for business success and tend to instead pursue opportunities that slow their careers.[5] But the executive women that I have interviewed who made it to the C-suite didn't focus on barriers; they knew where they were heading and focused on deliberately choosing a path to get them to their goal of leadership even if it appeared circuitous, being careful not to take a position that would not advance their capability, knowledge, and visibility. Savvy women on their way to power have a plan and they know what each step along the way will gain them.

Sandra, a VP of marketing, told me about how she negotiated with upper management before taking an assignment. "I told them, 'My only concern is that this is a staff job, not a line job. I want to get back into management, so I need some confirmation that by coming into this staff job that it doesn't close off a path for me. If it does, I don't want to do it.'"

Findings show that being "promoted" to special assignments that were outside the typical management path often blocked women's career advancement. So if women do not personally manage their career progression, they can get derailed.[6] But it takes savvy to see the value or cost of certain positions. Mary Barra showed this savvy by taking some staff positions that would gain her experience and credibility needed to get to top operational jobs. She took the director of communications job to "fix a troubled internal communications department" and took the role of VP of human resources to "bring efficiency to a messy HR department." Her appointment to lead HR made outsiders "scratch their heads" because they saw her as a horse in the race for the top job and wondered if this move was going to sideline her. But she and her executive peers knew that HR was going to be a strategic and critical function for the company at that point in time, and it was in desperate need of a "turnaround." And as we discussed before, a rigorous and defining proving ground for up and coming executives is taking an area of the company that is in trouble and fixing it.

Taking a line role with operations responsibility is seen as more valuable to career progression than taking a staff role, as Sandra knew. In fact, in a 2012 *Wall Street Journal* report, about 94 percent of S&P CEOs held key operations positions immediately before getting to the top job. But of the women in executive committee roles, that is, roles one level away from CEO, only one third of them were in operational positions. Two thirds of executive women in that group were in staff roles such as HR, communications, or legal.[7] Women tend toward, or are encouraged toward, staff roles. Line jobs carry greater pressure and are less flexible than staff jobs, potentially making staff jobs more appealing to those with family responsibilities. Also leaders may be reluctant to ask those with family responsibilities to take on those line roles, assuming they wouldn't be able to shoulder a tough assignment. And let's not ignore the obvious stereotyping of support positions being "feminine" roles. So for women who are mapping a career path to the top, staff roles can be a big detour, or worse. But not all staff roles are dead ends, as evidenced by Mary Barra's career path.

We see from previous chapters that successful executive women are very astute about the culture and the "lay of the land" so that they can effectively navigate it. They are aware of their audience and manage gender expectations by filing down the edges of male leadership characteristics. They temper assertiveness to couch their subject *mastery* and conceptual thinking skills. And we know if they didn't do this they would find themselves behind that brick wall of "bitch." Perhaps that is why research shows that women focus their leadership development on finding their niche and integrating themselves with the environment rather than focus on the mastery of more specific business skills as men do.[8]

Being savvy about culture and the lay of the land, successful executive women know that, in order to develop and advance, they can't just have a goal and pick the steppingstones to get there: They need mentors to pave the way for them. And their perspective on the people who help them advance is quite different from men's. Whereas men trust the system, assuming "some anonymous benefactor" in senior management will sponsor their advancement, women are quite aware of their "path paver," and know that that person will take risks for them. Women never assume that the system will take care of them.[9]

Successful women are particularly adept at recognizing who is "on their side" rooting for them and who is not. As we know from a previous chapter, their ability to see connections helps them figure out "who's who in the zoo," understanding the power dynamics and who has influence. But also, they are tuned in to the emotional nuances of people; able to read into the nonverbal cues that broadcast how another person is reacting to them. With their influencing skills, women can then connect to the people who both have sway in the organization and want them to succeed.

Successful executive women that I've interviewed all had mentors who helped their career development even though these women demonstrated the self-development savvy to plan their own route toward their career goal. So the roles of their mentors were not necessarily to model how to act in the environment, teach the ropes, and coach on performance. They provided visibility, developmental job opportunities, and promotional advocacy. Their mentors were actually sponsors.

The CFO of a large drug company credited the chutzpah of her mentor, Bill, for propelling her to her C-suite role. She said:

"I think he's gender blind. He was the one to stand tall for my big promotion. When I was made treasurer, there was a lot of resistance by the old boy's network. When my name was put forward, they were saying, 'Oh, you'll upset all the other men who are working in the area' and 'How can *she* be the treasurer?' So Bill finally said, 'We're doing it.' That kind of backbone and support is priceless. And once I made it past treasurer, there were no more naysayers."

Coming at this from another angle, I interviewed Tom, the COO of a Fortune 50 company, who told me about the sponsoring component of mentoring: "You have to have certain abilities to get ahead. Its all relationship oriented at a certain level; it's who you know. You must have someone at every level in your career to pull you along. So I did for Susan what other people have done for me. She's extremely competent, one of the most intelligent people I've ever met. So I pushed her and pulled her through the organization." He went on to proudly say that she is now the CEO of one of their spinoff companies. He earnestly wanted me to know that sponsoring is what it is all about. He said, "Any executive who tells you they got to the top on the basis of their abilities is being deceptive. It's a lie. They got there because someone pulled them up."

In the next chapter, I will address more fully how mentoring is different for men and women, and the complications that women and their male mentors have to navigate to have a successful, productive relationship. And I will talk about the complications that senior women face in being mentors to other women.

Self-development savvy doesn't help women leaders to break though "bitch," but it is a way to compensate for a system that doesn't do a good job of supporting their advancement, which is another brick wall. It is how successful women drive their progression to the C-suite: by having a goal, and figuring out which positions and experiences will lead to that goal, and which positions are a ticket to nowhere. It is also the savvy to build relationships with those who have influence and will market one's capabilities and potential. Finding that sponsor gives women the benefit that has so often advantaged their male colleagues; it hooks them into the well-established network of executive connections, traditionally referred to as the "old boys' club," that will pull them to the top.

PART THREE

Using the Road Map to Develop Leaders

CHAPTER 10

Helping Women Break Through the Barrier

Mentoring is critical to the development of leaders, particularly women[1], yet there are complications associated with mentoring women. Many men—who make up the majority of the mentor pool—are, to put it bluntly, uncomfortable with their female colleagues in these kinds of situations. Another obstacle is the unfortunate reality that women in leadership often do not help other women join them at the top of the corporate ladder. Thirty years of workplace evolution have not removed these inconvenient truths. Successful women leaders understand the specific reasons for men's discomfort with women and the ways to mitigate them, even if it is outside their full awareness. Mitigating the discomfort of both men and women is the essence of the Women's Leadership Blueprint. Successful women know how to garner the sponsorship of executive men in the C-suite. And despite the complexity of reasons that women don't advocate for other women, successful female leaders know how to use their power to sponsor women, without being labeled a "flag-waving feminist" or a "bitch."

Early Male Role Models

Women in the C-suite whom I have interviewed often credit family members, particularly male family members, as being critical to their success. They speak of grandfather, father, brother, and uncle as people who were, in the words of one woman, "largely responsible for where I am today." These men encouraged curiosity and confidence in the women when they were young; they included them in activities that might usually be reserved for boys (e.g., going fishing; playing catch in the backyard; going to a football game; creating a stock market portfolio). This has also been seen in other research on critical experiences that ready women for C-suite roles.[2]

I remember walking into the office of the CFO of a Fortune 100 company and being impressed with an antique that I thought might be an old clock. It had brass gears mounted on a round wooden platform and a glass bell over the ensemble. I saw what looked like a cloth tape measure originating from a wheel inside the glass bell and fed through the bottom lip of the glass. Ah, of course, a CFO would have an old ticker tape machine in her office. I didn't comment on it when I walked in, but toward the end of the interview when I asked her to tell me about important milestones in her career history she mentioned it right away.

She said:

"My grandfather is my role model. He was the owner of that little ticker tape. He was a lawyer but also an investor and he and I seemed to hit it off at an early age; he taught me how to read a stat page when I was 7, and stuff like that. And he talked to me about American history and about economics and I was always treated as an equal. He gave me an orientation toward business and the stock market, quite frankly."

The family members that executive women talked about generally showed them how to be viable in a man's world—how to be "one of the guys," how to gain acceptance in the male world, how to make men comfortable with them as peers. In this way, these early male influences were mentors. In stark contrast, none of the executive men I've interviewed mentioned family as critical to their success. In fact, one of the men I interviewed had a father who was CEO of his company years ago; not even he mentioned his father in any capacity, much less as a mentor!

Why do you suppose men didn't mention these male family influences as positioning them for career success? Maybe, admitting that a personal relationship had a profound impact on one's career success is a personal disclosure that perhaps the executive women felt more comfortable sharing. Men also may have felt more reluctant to admit that their success was associated with anything other than their own hard work, an apparently common foible of executive men, as I will point out in the next section. Still another explanation may be that the executive men did not have the same salient experience as the women did of having been given a special privilege; as males they may have simply expected the male family support. And after all, how to be one of the boys isn't something that boys have to specially learn; it just naturally comes with growing up as a male.

One C-suite executive woman, Lee, said that her father was a huge support, telling her, "You can do anything you want." Other successful female executives recounted the exact same story! Their fathers encouraged them to step up to the plate—sometimes literally—and they spoke up for their daughters to make sure they had equal membership with the boys. In this way, their fathers were their earliest sponsors.

Another executive woman, who had a brother who connected her with the boys' world, told me that she thought these relationships taught her how to have close, platonic relationships with men, a critical skill that I will discuss later in this chapter.

Later Mentoring Relationships

Some women have been lucky enough to be exposed to the guys' world through early male relationships. But what about those who haven't? For both those who have and those who have not, later relationships play a much more prominent role in an executive's advancement and professional development. And women particularly gain value from establishing these relationships, because there is no large hand coming out of a cloud from the C-suite to pull them up the ladder.

A few executive men I interviewed talked about having mentors who were prominent in their advancement, but for the most part it was the successful executive women who proactively cultivated a relationship with powerful people. As mentioned earlier, men seem to trust the system assuming that "some anonymous bene-factor" in senior management sponsored their advance-ment.[3] Tom, a COO mentioned in an earlier chapter, supported this, saying he thought a lot of male C-suite executives portray, and think of, themselves as a "self-made man." Tom was the person who tuned me into this C-suite male foible. But he himself thought otherwise.

Tom said, "Men get the CEO job and believe everything in their press release. They think they are all knowing, no need to learn or get help. Women CEOs are more willing to be flexible and collaborative."

Executive women, even those exposed to early influential male relationships, talk about the value of a mentor to teach them how to play in a man's world.

Executive women, even those exposed to early influ-ential male relationships, talk about the value of a mentor to teach them how to play in a man's world. For example, Lee grew up among three brothers, said she was "a bit of a tomboy." and always felt a part of the male group, yet she still wobbled a bit when bullied by her male execu-tive counterparts. She recounted, "I was in a high visibil-ity position and my male peers were being adversarial, 'playing hard ball.'" She went to her mentor practically in tears. He said to her, "If you want to run with the big dogs, you have to be a big dog." He proceeded to advise her on how to do just that. So even though Lee had learned how to "play ball" with the boys early in life, it wasn't quite enough to be able to run with the "big dogs." Lee's mentor bolstered her confidence to make her male colleagues "stand down"; it was the affirmation she needed.

Women need the advocacy and additional leverage that a highly placed mentor provides more than men do. And if a woman wants to advance in her career she must find an appropriate mentor and establish a relationship.[4] Because of the relative dearth of executive women in the C-suite, a woman seeking career advancement often must find a mentor who is a man.

Successful executive women start early to look for those who will sponsor them through the obstacle course of the organization's political landscape. Sharon, the VP of a global electronics firm, told me that when she joined the company, she spent her first few weeks meeting with the CEO and business unit heads. "I wanted to meet with each of them individually, without a formal agenda, to build rapport and understand what they wanted from my function. I wanted to understand who would be supportive and sponsor my work," she said. Sharon added, "I've always had key sponsors along my career. A sponsor is someone who will support me and support my work when I'm not in the room." Then she reflected, "They identify projects for you to lead and put you out in front. But you can't just approach someone and ask him or her to sponsor you. You need to find who already supports you and then acknowledge it." Sharon "closes the deal" by thanking her identified sponsor for supporting her work. She keeps him or her updated on the progress of her initiatives and any obstacles she has encountered. Without asking, her sponsor then works the management committee to shake loose those obstacles.

Why Can't a Woman Be More Like a Man?

Poor Professor Higgins! He's "just an ordinary man... who likes to live his life free of strife.... But let a woman in your life your serenity is through." So befuddled by women—so uncomfortable! One of the less-talked-about issues that impact women's advancement to executive positions is that men can simply be uncomfortable with women. This lack of comfort creates a need for women to behave in ways that make men more comfortable with them. Successful executive women have broken through this discomfort by "filing down the sharp edges" of assertiveness, confidence, and command of their expertise. So by breaking through "bitch," that wall erected to keep out the "abrasive and intimidating" female, successful women have taken a significant step in easing the tension and discomfort of men. They have established common ground, building rapport, creating a platform to engage in casual conversation, and allowing their male colleagues to get to know them and understand the way they think and operate. Even poor ol' Henry Higgins might say, as he does of men, "Whenever you're with them, you're always at ease."

Executive women's ability to create common ground and develop a solid relationship with their male colleagues addresses one of the reasons for men's discomfort with women: fear of straying from what is known—and what is known is how men, not women, run the organization. Women are still perceived as "risky" appointments for C-suite roles, appointments made by male-dominated committees.[5] An executive man I interviewed said, "The old boys' club is afraid to change from what they know works." In other words, women will do things differently, and in doing things differently from how it has worked in the past, it may not work as well.

Consistent with the discomfort of promoting women to these high-profile positions, but *not* with the speculation that it's because of a fear of the unknown, is a study of top-performing CEOs. The women chief executives in the study were twice as likely as men to have been hired from outside the company! So a woman inside the company—*a known entity*—is less likely than a man to be promoted to the top spot.[6] That would argue that it isn't a fear of the unknown that is driving the old boys' club to be afraid of changing what they know works. Is it really back to the issue that there are not enough women inside the company who have managed to break through "bitch"—the women who have had the chance to build a reputation and track record? Are women outside the company, during the relatively short recruiting process, better able to break through that wall because they don't have a company history where people know their warts as an emerging leader?

Some researchers suggest that men feel uncomfortable because they are less experienced in dealing with women as professional colleagues and peers, and that some executive men only know women in the context of wife, mother, daughter, secretary, or lover. I might put it a bit differently and point out that most men working at the executive level have stay-at-home wives. So in their current circumstances most executive men's primary female relationship fits that predominant stereotype of tending the home front (meaning *not* the work front). When I say most, let me be clear: When I worked at a large management consulting firm as a principal, *all* of my male colleagues had stay-at-home spouses, and some of the female principals with children also had stay-at-home spouses. I am in no way implying that this is a bad thing. It's just a reality that frames how particularly men view women in the workplace.

But my research indicates there is even more to the story, and it goes back to something mentioned earlier in this chapter about the importance of learning how to have close, platonic relationships with men. Yes, we are going there! Successful executive women have figured out how to navigate the murky waters of sexual attraction.

Both male and female executives suggest that another component of men's discomfort with women is sexual tension—yes, that thing we don't like to talk about. I asked an executive woman if she experienced any sexual tensions in mentoring relationships, and she said, "I'll tell you about it—off the record." Women observed that this sexual tension might be reduced if a woman is "not attractive" or is married or is made gender "invisible." But successful executive women—attractive or not—have found a way to trump this important dilemma by "keeping things light." As with so many other things, women use humor to cut through tension. If sexual tension is at the root of men's discomfort though, women may have a difficult time finding a mentor and getting sponsorship.

In describing how he finds people that he wishes to mentor, one executive emphasized personal chemistry, trust, and a similar value system. It struck me how similar this was to how one might describe the attraction to a romantic/sexual partner. Given the personal nature of the criteria and the close bond that often comes with a mentoring relationship, it's not surprising that there could be welcomed or unwelcomed sexual tension in a mentoring relationship between a heterosexual man and woman.

Sexual tension may be a real issue for mentoring in general and for women especially. One male in the C-suite told me that, as an executive, it is important to be married! Although he framed the importance of having a spouse as a social necessity, it seemed like the underlying reason was that married people are less of a sexual threat than non-married people. This could be equally true for mentor or protégé.

In a predominantly heterosexual world where most potential mentors are men, successful executive women have not only had to manage their career and find a mentor, but also have had to manage the difficulties of mutual or non-mutual, welcomed or unwelcomed, sexual attraction!

One executive woman speculated that if she had been more attractive, men would have been uncomfortable with her, and she would not have advanced to the

C-suite. True or not, she perceived that there is a potential danger to one's career if sexual attraction is an issue. A male CEO told me that executive men's wives are very distrustful of executive women. He also mentioned that none of those wives work outside the home. Lack of trust might come from the tension between women who have put their career on hold, or have decided to focus on home and family, and women who have advanced in their career to the highest levels. But really, the unspoken implication for executive wives' mistrust of their husbands' female colleagues is that female colleagues could be, or become, a romantic connection. So is it any wonder that some executive men would think it much easier just to "stay away"? But for an executive woman dealing with this issue, she can't just simply "stay away" without jeopardizing her career success. The jealousy of spouses, an obstacle existing well beyond the C-suite, is yet another potential hurdle for executive women to gracefully leap over.

Research on the career-enhancing relationships of men and women indicates that women's immediate bosses were not likely to be their mentors because "even rumors of sexual involvement could damage the careers of both mentor and subordinate."[7] Rumors of inappropriate behavior are evident in the *New York Times* story of an executive man who replaced his wooden office door with a glass one. His reason was that he wanted to stop rumors about "improprieties" between himself and his 27-year-old, female protégé. Wisely, he said, "Better a glass door than a glass ceiling."[8] If women only have limited access to their bosses and mentors because they are worried that people may see the relationship as inappropriately sexual; it puts women at a significant disadvantage from their male counterparts. Seldom do we hear an accusation, much less speculation, that a male protégé slept his way to the top!

Sheryl Sandberg told a story in her book, *Lean In*, about working with Larry Summers. They were traveling together and one night were preparing for a presentation the next day. They were working in his hotel suite. She said that when they were calling it quits for the night, she noticed that it was 3:00 am. She said, "We both knew it would look awful if anyone saw me leaving his hotel suite at that time." He thought he could check first and make sure no one was in the hallway. She said, "Then we realized we were stuck because there is no difference between trying not to be seen leaving someone's hotel room late at night and *actually* leaving someone's hotel room late at night. I strode into the (luckily) empty hall and made it to my room undetected."

Even when an executive man *does* mentor a woman, he may be reluctant to play the sponsorship role, essentially broadcasting the relationship by publicly advocating for her. And research does shows that while women are being mentored, often they are not being sponsored.[9] And not being sponsored means slower and fewer promotions.

It was interesting to hear a frank admission about sexual attraction between mentor and protégé—from a female mentor's point of view. She confided a mutual attraction between herself and a male protégé. She spoke of the difficulty of managing the relationship because the attention was so flattering and affirming that it was difficult not to get too caught up in it. No executive men talked to me about sexual attraction to a protégé, but they must also find it quite flattering to have the attention and interest of a smart, young woman. Who wouldn't be attracted to that kind of flattery! However compelling, the sexual tension can be detrimental; a one-sided sexual attraction—of mentor toward protégé—might lead to misunderstandings and potential sexual harassment charges.[10]

In a study about mentoring relationships, two factors— "same sex easier" and "public image"—came up most often and were closely associated with each other. This again shows that women themselves worry about how a relationship with a male mentor would be publicly received.

These sexual tension or attraction issues create difficulties for a woman seeking a mentoring relationship that are generally not present for a man. If she is not married or is attractive, she can be seen as a sexual threat and therefore a risk to a potential mentor. If she spends too much time with her mentor, she can be the fodder of office gossip that could damage her reputation and cause others to take her less seriously. If her mentor is attracted to her, she has to manage the relationship carefully in order to gain the career benefits without encouraging or offending her mentor. In the worst case, she must cope with a mentor who is attracted to her and who uses or threatens to use his power inappropriately to solicit a favorable response from her.

Because the mentor/protégé relationship is so critical to women's success, executive women have worked through the issues of male-female mentoring relationships. How have they done it? They ensure that their persona is non-sexual—in the way they act, in the way they dress, in what they say and how they say it. And remarkably, they do this without sacrificing their basic femininity. Executive women that I've interviewed have come across as feminine, even those who said they—or their male colleagues—identified them as tomboys. Some wear makeup, some don't; some have polished nails, some don't; some wear skirts, some don't. They are being their feminine selves while maintaining a personal brand that doesn't promote sexuality.

I attended an academic conference of organizational psychologists where an HR executive presented results of a leadership development program that she had developed. The work was brilliant, but that wasn't what was remarkable. She was tall and slim, and wore a closely tailored, partially opened blouse and a tight white skirt that just barely covered her butt! She was on a stage at the front of the room, so this was definitely *not* a great choice of wardrobe. But apparently, she was known for dressing this way when she made a presentation. A female colleague sitting next to me leaned over and whispered, "I'm straight and this woman has *me* thinking about sex!" Suffice it to say, the presenter's personal brand exuded sexuality.

The previous example is extreme, and there are more subtle cues that can amp up sexuality. But in the example, the presenter could have worn a professional outfit without sacrificing her femininity. The feat that successful women have achieved—largely by erasing sexuality from the situation—is that they can build close relationships with men that are platonic. For some, they come by it naturally, without having to try. Others make a conscious effort to neutralize their sexuality.

Women Who Don't Help Other Women

Madeleine Albright has said—and the late, great Ann Richards, former governor of Texas, has echoed—"There's a special place in hell for women who don't help other women."

One executive man I interviewed was adamant that women not helping other women is the key problem for women's advancement. He said:

> "Women are very critical of other women. They don't seem willing to mentor and role model other women, and certainly don't create an appropriate pull together.... I sometimes get the feeling that women that make it to the top of a company say, 'I got here; you get here. I fought all the stereotypes; I put up with the bullshit, so you do it too. Why should I help you? Nobody helped me.' I have several examples in mind where I've seen that occur."

This is a phenomenon that has been observed and documented for a long time. Twenty years ago, there were worried discussions that the competition among women in business was "the last remaining conversational taboo because it reinforced damaging sexist stereotypes."[11] Rosabeth Moss Kanter said that the perception that there are limited positions for women at the top cause women to compete directly for scarce status and power.[12]

Sheryl Sandberg discussed in her book that even in 2013 there was still a perceived competition among women for a limited opportunity, referring to it as the "there can be only one" attitude. The Queen Bee syndrome persists as a result of a patriarchal work culture where comparatively few women rise to the top. And where there is a perception that "eager talent trumps experience," accomplished women may be reluctant to "give away all the secrets to their success" to a younger, eager female talent.[13] Wittingly or unwittingly, there are women who are holding back other women.

Janet, a 38-year-old SVP at a tech company, told me a story about a woman who was her boss a few years ago, which unfortunately reinforces the "I fought hard to get here. I'm not going to make it easy on you" attitude. Her boss told her, "I've gotten accolades about you, and I just don't get it. You are so arrogant." Clearly her boss didn't like her style, and didn't like hearing how well respected and liked Janet was in the company. Janet found out later that this woman "got rid of" other competent women and eventually was fired for her behavior. I think it's safe to imagine where this woman would go if Ann Richards had her wish.

But let's not be too quick to think the worst of all women who haven't helped other women. As we've seen from Catalyst research, experienced women with status are mentoring other women, but aren't necessarily sponsoring other women. Although this has been attributed to women's competition with other women, I don't buy it. Rosabeth Moss Kanter observed that women who reach executive status simply feel obligated to distance themselves from other women. And based on my research, I would agree.

I interviewed several women who were on the executive committee of a Fortune 500 company who said that they had a female colleague who was also a member of the top management team but that she did not have a relationship with that female colleague. Each woman expressed a desire to forge a relationship with the other woman on the team, but felt in some way that the other woman did not welcome it!

So, there appears to be a stigma attached to women building connections with other women. Interestingly, one executive man observed, "Men are already acculturated for corporate life; women have to become acculturated." This may explain why there is a stigma attached to forming a network or bond with other women. Once a woman has "made it" and joined the upper echelons of the old boys' club, she may have to distance herself from other women to preserve her credibility and to indicate that she has acculturated to executive male society. Likewise, a woman who is working toward an executive role may feel that, in order to gain credibility, she must distance herself from her female counterparts. In this way, she can demonstrate that she is different, is not a part of the female culture, and is willing to acculturate to executive male society.[14] They don't want to dilute that credibility by seeming to have a "feminist agenda."

Diana, head of HR for a large insurance company, said to me that she was tired of sitting at the table with her peers—all men—working on succession planning, without a single woman's name coming up. She said that as the only woman reporting to the CEO, she couldn't be the one "waving the flag" in support of promoting women into leadership. What she did do, however, was work with my team on a women's leadership program for the top 45 women managers. On the second day of the event, the women were given a board directive business challenge—to break into a particular new market. The group divided themselves into teams and took on different aspects of planning the project. At the end of the day, they reported to the two SVPs of operations, and were received with enthusiasm. The work was a yearlong initiative that resulted in three women being promoted to senior leadership roles. Diana was able to create a situation where she essentially—though indirectly—sponsored a group of women, without being seen as the one woman on the executive committee advocating for women.

In a women's leadership conference that we facilitated, this issue of upper-level women not connecting with their female peers came up spontaneously in conversation. It turned into a comic relief moment when one woman in the room related an incident where she was "seen in the hallway 'congregating' with another senior-level woman" and how a male peer reacted nervously and said (you can guess), "What are you two up to?" Yes, when two or more women are together, it must mean trouble!

As a research scientist in the mid-1980s, I was very much a part of a male-dominated culture that started from the time I was in college. I worked very hard to be "one of the guys" and not show any obvious affiliation with other women. I wanted to demonstrate affiliation with the male culture. Sadly, I was not the only woman in school, or in R&D at a large pharmaceutical company, who acted that way. My company held a special event for all of the women across the organization. It was the first time such an event took place. I was not surprised that many of my female science colleagues complained that they "didn't have time for that [expletive]." They framed it as a waste of time, and I suppose that was part of the reason for their rejection of the event, as they placed no value on "connecting as women." But I suspect that, like me at that time, the main reason for their rejection was that they didn't want the guys to ridicule them for partaking in some silly social function for women, and more importantly, to see them as breaking ranks.

Breaking through the barriers to development requires some in-depth understanding of all of the gender dynamics at play. Although organizations themselves need to remove barriers to women's success, there is much that women can do in spite of the barriers.

Successful executive women have created a persona that makes their male counterparts feel comfortable.

Successful executive women have created a persona that makes their male counterparts feel comfortable. They have achieved this first, by gaining a comfort level with the male culture, which may happen as a result of supportive and encouraging relationships with male family members; second, by operating within a range of acceptable behavior that includes the best female stereotypic qualities and the best qualities of the white male leadership culture; third, by reducing the likelihood that one may be seen as a sexual threat; and finally, by being seen as a credible acculturated member of the male leadership culture. The Women's Leadership Blueprint describes the set of behaviors that have allowed these executive women to do all this, helping them to develop and advance to the top.

CHAPTER 11

What's Good for the Goose Is Good for the Gander

Women are not the only ones who can benefit by developing the behaviors described in this book. Though women leaders benefit by breaking through "bitch" and men don't need to worry about that, today's organizations need leaders who are skilled in these collaborative skills, both women and men. Warren Bennis, an expert on organizational leadership, called this an egalitarian age that requires a new style of leader. Organizations are knowledge-based and highly automated. So leaders need to be coaches to leverage knowledge workers, rather than colonels whose autocratic, directive style risks alienating those talented resources. Companies are more matrixed, organized by project, product, or process rather than by hierarchical chains of command. Leaders in these environments must depend on their power of influence. Enterprises of all sorts are working to increase innovation, as evident in a whole industry that has emerged to advise organizations on increasing creativity and innovation. Leaders have to let go of power to open those creative channels. Businesses are facing a new economic environment in which they need different approaches to increase productivity, to stimulate growth, and to engage their people. Leaders cannot just do what has traditionally worked in the past.

Collaborative leadership is the wave of the future, and it is what is working now. Traditional leaders have depended on their position of authority, have only shared information on a "need to know" basis, and were the ones who came up with the solutions. Collaborative leaders share the power and information with their team, stimulating collective problem-solving and allowing solutions to develop from the best ideas of the group. This distribution of power among group members grows trust and is associated with innovation and increased team performance[1], and with releasing untapped talent and increasing engagement.[2]

What does it take to be a collaborative leader? The Women's Leadership Blueprint describes the competencies that are the hallmarks of this style of leadership. And there are common behavioral themes that come up throughout the nine competencies. What helps women break through "bitch" can also provide a path to success for male leaders, and ultimately, lead to more successful organizations.

Empathy

Empathy allows leaders to relate to others. Their ability to sense what others are feeling helps them identify connections with peers and higher-ups and results in having a strong ability to influence. Building these strategic connections with other leaders has been shown to foster broader, "big picture thinking" and lead to "radical creativity" among employees.[3] Radical creativity is the ability to develop useful, novel ideas that differ from the status quo. Research shows that this is critical for sustainable innovation in organizations.[4]

By showing their empathy, leaders build emotional connections with their employees; they help establish emotional bonds among employees, creating a sense of team and belonging. This sense of community, where people feel allied with others to pursue a collective goal, creates the psychological safety and motivation for people to offer their ideas.[5]

Empathetic leaders build trust and facilitate information-sharing, both necessary components of leading and managing change.

Self-Awareness

Great leaders are in touch with their feelings and those of others, and use those emotions as data to guide decisions and facilitate conflict resolution. Self-aware leaders understand how they are being perceived, and therefore they know how to modify their behavior so that others can relate to them and engage with them.

Inclusiveness

Leaders who are democratic and involve others bring together their teams to engage in problem-solving and kicking around ideas. This goes beyond gathering input and getting buy in to move an agenda forward. Leaders come to the table with their teams to figure out what is the best solution; they do not assume that they have the best answer. So in addition to collecting valuable information from a wide scope of people, inclusive leaders gain the intellectual horsepower of their people. And in an environment where people are hired for their knowledge and capabilities, it makes good business sense to actually tap into what they are being paid for.

Erasing Hierarchical Boundaries

Establishing Common Ground

In order to put people at ease, leaders do a variety of things that diminish hierarchy and the boundaries it creates. They work to establish a common ground between themselves and others in the organization, providing a platform to have casual conversation about mutual interests and create rapport. These connections balance differences in level so a CEO and a frontline employee can relate to each other without the awkwardness associated with being on very different rungs of the ladder. But importantly, these casual relationships permeate the organization providing channels up, down, and across for sharing information and ideas.

Having an Egalitarian Mind-Set

Great leaders make their audience feel smart *with* them, rather than feel intimidated *by* them. They assume that people can keep up with them and, by doing so, they erase any air of superiority. Egalitarian-oriented leaders create a persona of relatability and approachability that facilitates people not being afraid to share their ideas.

Thinking "We," not "I"

In a world without hierarchy, the pronoun "I" goes by the wayside and "we" is the order of the day. Successful collaborative leaders frame their achievements as team efforts. They believe it is the power of the team that produces the results. They share power to distribute decision-making and to engage their teams to feel like owners in the enterprise. By sharing power, a collaborative leader profoundly and positively influences the culture, creating an atmosphere for ideas to form and flourish.

Letting Others Take the Lead

Ultimately it is the leader who carries responsibility for the results of their organization. Collaborative leadership is no different. For those in the C-suite, it is true that "the buck stops here," but successful leaders have the ability to empower others while retaining control of critical initiatives. They focus delegates on understanding exactly what they want to achieve, then allow them to proceed to achieve it. Collaborative leaders delegate such that the delegates feel they are leading the charge and that the leader is coaching and guiding them. They maintain the power and responsibility of their leadership position while being seen as a partner in achieving results.

Cultural and Political Savvy

Successful leaders are astute in grasping a culture or a group dynamic and figuring out how to best use that understanding to take effective action. They know how to navigate the political environment and relationships that form the power network of the organization, and help their teams understand the best routes to take. Collaborative leaders use their savvy to fit in and adapt as the climate changes. They help their people understand the underlying meaning behind actions and how the team fits in to the organization's big picture.

But leaders also impact the culture of their organization. Collaborative leaders model the behaviors described here and throughout this book. They set a tone and cause others to behave in a way that is consistent with what they see and experience from their leaders. These behaviors create a culture that allows innovation to blossom, nurtures development of people and teams, and creates engagement.

Communicating Insights and Vision

In a new economy that needs a new way of doing business, successful leaders take a broad, long-range view of the world and see trends that will impact their organization. They are influential by virtue of their ability to think big and think outside the box, and have the cognitive horsepower to gain credibility with their teams. They "connect the dots," making meaning out of a jumble of voluminous information. Importantly, collaborative leaders share their insights in a simple, straightforward way so others can readily understand them. And in doing this, not only are they inspiring a broad range of people, they are reducing the intimidation factor that can crop up when faced with a visionary leader. There is nothing like intimidation to freeze people's creative thinking and willingness to share ideas. Collaborative leaders spark others to think "outside the box."

In striving toward innovation, today's organizations benefit from creating a culture that emphasizes risk-taking and openness to ideas, which leads to the creation of new products, new services, new markets, new customers, and new opportunities. The leaders who nurture these budding ideas are those who build trust by demonstrating empathy, self-awareness, inclusiveness, and cultural and political savvy; erasing hierarchy; and communicating insights and vision.

Women who made it to the C-suite did it by filing down the sharp edges of traditional male leadership. They "feminized" leadership to overcome the barriers of gender expectations—to break through "bitch." When we look at those behaviors associated with their success, and see the results that they generate, we realize that women may have shown us what it takes to be a great leader of innovation.

Much research is underway to understand what it takes to lead innovation. Of particular interest is a book by Linda Hill[6], professor at the Harvard Business School, that describes various situations illustrative of sustained innovation and the leaders who create that environment. Also, a thoughtful book-length essay by Ed Catmull[7], president of Pixar Animation and Disney Animation, spells out the tensions of maintaining a culture of innovation. What struck me most as I read both of these was how very well suited the Women's Leadership Blueprint is to leading innovation. A further testimony to that is when I spoke briefly with Greg Brandeau, longtime head of technology at Pixar Animation. I told him about my research findings on women leaders and asked if research had been done to understand the composite characteristics of leaders at Pixar. After saying that no study had been done, he leaned forward, as if sharing a confidence, and said, "But most of the leaders at Pixar are women."

So, given all this, I say: What's good for the goose is good for the gander.

APPENDIX

Perceptions of the Goose and Gander: Importance of the Women's Leadership Blueprint

The Women's Leadership Blueprint allows women to break through "bitch." But it also allows both women and men to lead innovation. Do leaders value these competencies as critical to their leadership success? Are some competencies more important than others? Do men and women value them differently? Have opinions changed since a decade ago?

Do leaders value these competencies as critical to their leadership success?
Yes.

In 2000, executives I interviewed participated in a survey to validate the competencies that are now part of the Women's Leadership Blueprint. The survey asked executives to rate the importance of each competency for their effectiveness as a leader. On a scale of 1 (not important) to 7 (critical) with the middle rating of 4 being important, the average rating for the competencies was 5.9, ranging from 6.5 to 4.3. Men and women in the C-suite valued this set of competencies as being very important for their effectiveness as a leader.

Later, in 2014, a diverse group of 100 senior executives also validated the importance of these competencies. Their average rating was 5.6, ranging from 6.0 to 5.0. In general, participants in 2014 rated the competencies somewhat lower that those in 2000. These differences can be a result of the demographics of the executives. In 2000, the executives were all at the C-suite level and gender balanced; in 2014, participants ranged from "leaders of managers" to "leaders of organizations," and only one-third of the participants were women. Interestingly, the leaders in this survey who were two or three tiers down from the chief executive level generally rated these competencies slightly lower than those leaders nearest the top. And not surprisingly, the women in the 2014 survey tended to rate the competencies higher than the men did.

Are some competencies more important than others?
Yes.

The influence competencies were the highest rated competencies in 2000 and 2014, with persuasion and inspiring commitment topping the charts. Self-development savvy, although one of the lower rated competencies, was rated significantly higher in 2014 than in 2000. Again, with some participants in 2014 not having reached the C-suite, self-development savvy could be more important to them, as they still could be charting a course to advance. (See Figure 1.)

Do men and women value the competencies differently?
Yes.

The differences between how men and women view the competencies are relatively small when combining the results from 2000 and 2014. The greatest difference

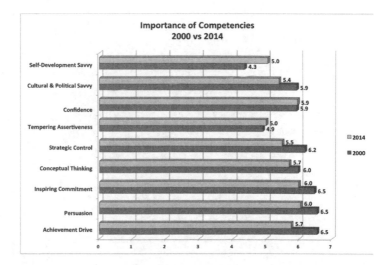

Figure 1. Importance of Competencies, 2000 vs. 2014.

was that women rated tempering assertiveness higher than men did, which is not surprising given it is a competency that most, if not all, successful women leaders demonstrate. Conceptual thinking and persuasion are also strengths that women leverage for leadership success, and women rated them higher in importance than men. (See Figure 2.)

Looking separately at women's perceptions in 2000 versus 2014 and men's perceptions in 2000 versus 2014, there are some interesting gender differences, particularly for three of the competencies. (See Figure 3.)

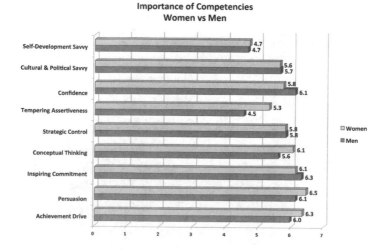

Figure 2. Importance of Competencies, Women vs. Men

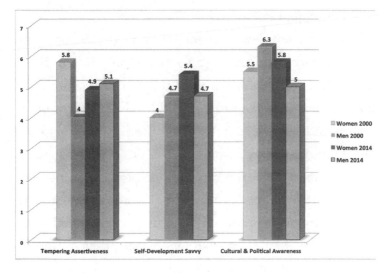

Figure 3. Importance of Competencies: Gender Difference
2000 vs. 2014

Tempering Assertiveness

Men see tempering assertiveness as more important to their leadership success in 2014, rating it 5.1, versus a rating of 4.0 in 2000. Women in 2014 rated this competency lower than they did in 2000 but rated it at about the same level as men in 2014. Whereas tempering assertiveness is a way for women to avoid intimidating people—to avoid "bitch"; men in 2014 see this competency as critical to their leadership effectiveness as well. In a more team-based work environment, leaders putting people at ease, which is the key result of tempering assertiveness, is an important ability for both women and men.

Self-Development Savvy

Women see self-development savvy as more important to their success in 2014 (5.4) than they did in 2000; and they see it as more important than men who rated it 4.7, in both 2000 and 2014. As discussed in this book, men have been able to trust the system to support their development whereas women have not, perhaps explaining why men rated the importance of this competency the same in both years. Meanwhile, women have become more aware of the importance to find mentors and sponsors, and to chart their own career, and their rating for this competency increased in 2014.

Cultural and Political Savvy

Women in 2014 place more importance on cultural and political savvy than men do, and they also rate it as somewhat more important in 2014 than women did in 2000. In 2000, the competency was defined in the same way but labeled "political awareness." Highlighting the cultural savvy aspect of this competency may have made it less important to men and more important to women. As discussed in this book, women are wary of corporate politics, and women leaders claim that knowledge of corporate politics has nothing to do with their success. They do, however, see that understanding and adapting to the culture are vital. Men, on the other hand, see political savvy as necessary to their success, but understanding and fitting into the culture, not so much.

Importance Ranking

When asked to rank order the competencies, women and men choose the same ones for their "top five," but in a different order. (See Figure 4.)

Men and women alike saw inspiring commitment as the most important leadership competency. From there, the competency ranking differed. The most striking difference was in the next highest ranking. Men ranked achievement drive as the second most important competency. Women, on the other hand, ranked persuasion second.

Top-Five-Ranked Most Important Competencies	
WOMEN	MEN
Inspiring Commitment	Inspiring Commitment
Persuasion	**Achievement Drive**
Confidence	Confidence
Conceptual Thinking	**Persuasion**
Achievement Drive	**Conceptual Thinking**

Table A-4

This finding is almost predictable when you consider what has been covered in this book about differences in how men and women lead. The drive to accomplish more, to be "the best" and achieve better results than anyone on earth has ever seen, has the markings of assertiveness, competitiveness, and independence and masterfulness. Those characteristics fit the male leadership stereotype, and may indeed be the harbinger of success for men. So it is not surprising that men ranked it as second most important while women did not. Women leaders know that achievement drive is an "in your face" competency that they need to finesse, and that there are other competencies that are more important for their effectiveness, such as persuasion.

Executive women ranked persuasion, the ability to "influence up," as the second-most-important competency, and research shows that it is a strength for women. It allows them to advance their agenda and be seen as collaborative. Their ranking also may indicate that they have a tougher sell to senior executives (than men do), and that achieving stellar results is not enough to be seen as an effective leader.

CHAPTER NOTES

Chapter 1

1. Heilman, M.E., Block, C.J., Martell, R.F., and Simon, M.C. (1988). "Has Anything Changed? Current Characterizations of Men, Women and Managers." *Journal of Applied Psychology 74(6)*: 935–42.
2. Kirchmeyer, C. (1998). "Determinants of Managerial Success: Evidence and Explanation of Male/Female Differences." *Journal of Management 24(6)*: 673–92.
3. Fisher, H. *The First Sex: The Natural Talents of Women and How They Are Changing the World* (New York: Ballantine Books, 2000).
4. Schiff, S. *Cleopatra: A Life* (New York: Little, Brown and Company, 2010).
5. Foreman, A. "The Special Vilification of Female Leaders." *The Wall Street Journal*, May 3–4, 2014.
6. "Tavistock Model." The New York Center for the Study of Groups, Organizations, and Social Systems Website. *www.nycgrouprelations.org/pdf/TavistockModel.pdf.*

7. Smith, K.K. *Groups in Conflict: Prisons in Disguise* (Dubuque, Iowa: Kendall / Hunt Publishing, 1982).

Smith, K.K., and Berg, D.N. *Paradoxes of Group Life* (San Francisco, Calif.: Jossey-Bass, 1987).

8. Nieva, V.F., and Gutek, B.A. (1980). "Sex Effects on Evaluation." *Academy of Management Review 5*: 267–76.

9. Lips, H. *Women, Men and the Psychology of Power* (Prentice-Hall, 1981).

10. Heilman, M.E. (1997). "Sex Discrimination and the Affirmative Action Remedy: The Role of Sex Stereotypes." *Journal of Business Ethics 16*: 877–89.

Lyness, K.S., and Thompson, D.E. (1997). "Above the Glass ceiling? A Comparison of Matched Samples of Female and Male Executives." *Journal of Applied Psychology, 82(3)*: 359–75.

Greenhaus, J.H., and Parasuraman, S. (1993). "Job Performance Attributes and Career Advancement Prospects: An Examination of Gender and Race Effects." *Organizational Behavior and Human Decision Processes 55*: 273–97.

Powell, G.N., and Mainiero, L.A. (1992). "Cross-Currents in the River of Time: Conceptualizing the Complexities of Women's Careers." *Journal of Management 18*: 215–37.

Eagly, A.H., Makhijani, M.G., and Klonsky, B.G. (1992). "Gender and the Evaluation of Leaders: A Meta-Analysis." *Psychologies Bulletin 111(1)*: 3–11.

Eagly, A.H., and Johnson, B.T. (1990). "Gender and Leadership Style: A Meta-Analysis." *Psychological Bulletin 108(2)*: 233–56.

Morrison, A.M., and von Glinow, M.A. (1990). "Women and Minorities in Management." *American Psychologist 45*: 200–8.

Geis, F.L., Carter, M.R., and Butler, D.J. *Seeing and Evaluating People* (217/5M/6-86/M) (Newark: University of Delaware, Office of Women's Affairs, 1986).

11. Nieva and Gutek (1980).
12. Heilman (1997).
13. Ibid.

Chapter 2

1. Reed, B.G. (1983). "Women Leaders in Small Groups: Social-Psychological Perspectives and Strategies." *Social Work With Groups 6*: 35–41.
2. Phelan, C.A., and Rudman, L.A. (April 2010). "Prejudice Toward Female Leaders: Backlash Effects and Women's Impression Management Dilemma." *Social and Personality Psychology Compass*: 807–20.

Chapter 3

1. Phelan and Rudman (2010); Kirchmeyer (1998); Heilman (1997); Eagly, Makhijani; and Klonsky (1992); Reed, (1983).

Van Velsor, E., and Hughes, M.W. "Gender Differences in the Development of Managers: How Women Managers Learn From Experience." Technical Report 145 (Greensboro, N.C.: Center for Creative Leadership, 1990).

Morrison, A.M., White, R.P., Van Velsor, E., and the Center for Creative Leadership. *Breaking the Glass Ceiling* (Reading, Mass.: Addison-Wesley, 1987).

2. Eagly, Makhijani, and Klonsky (1992).

Eagly, A.H., Johannesen-Schmidt, M., and Van Engen, M. (2003). "Transformational, Transactional, and Laissez Faire Leadership Styles: A Meta-Analysis Comparing Men and Women." *Psychological Bulletin 129(4)*: 569–91.

3. Hay McBer. "Mastering Global Leadership: Hay/McBer International CEO Leadership Study" (Boston, Mass.: Hay, 1995).

Spencer, L.M., and Spencer, S.M. *Competence at Work* (New York: John Wiley and Sons, 1993).

Spencer, L.M., McClelland, D.C., and Spencer, S.M. *Competency Assessment Methods* (Boston: Hay/McBer Research, 1990).

Boyatzis, R.E. *The Competent Manager: A Model for Effective Performance* (New York: John Wiley, 1982).

4. Van Velsor and Hughes (1990).

McCauslan, J.A., and Kleiner, B.H. (1992). "Women and Organizational Leadership." *Equal Opportunities International 11(6)*: 12–15.

Chapter 4

1. Rosener, J.B. "Ways Women Lead." Harvard Business Review, November–December 1990, 119–25.
2. Terri Kelly's interview: *www.mixhackathon.org/video/terri-kelly-are-you-ready-give-power-get-results-1.*
3. Interview quotes by Mary Barra: *www.gsb.stanford.edu/news/headlines/quotable-mary-barra.*
4. Van Velsor and Hughes (1990).
5. Interview with Marissa Mayer: *www.makers.com/marissa-mayer.*

Chapter 5

1. "Women Poised to Effectively Lead in Matrix Work Environments." Hay Report, March 27, 2012. Study based on Hay Group's Emotional and Social Competency Inventory database that includes information from more than 17,000 individuals.
2. Grant, A. "The Dark Side of Emotional Intelligence." *The Atlantic*, January 2, 2014.
3. Eagly, A.H., and Johannesen-Schmidt, M. (2001). "The Leadership Styles of Women and Men." *Journal of Social Issues 57(4)*: 781–97.
4. Eagly, Makhijani, and Klonsky (1992).
5. Rosener (1990).
6. Phelan and Rudman (2010).

Chapter 6

1. Fisher (2000).
2. Ibid.
3. Ibid.
4. "Whatever women do, they must do twice as well as men to be thought half as good. Luckily, this is not difficult." From Charlotte Whitton, first female mayor in Canada.

Chapter 7

1. Kotter, J.P., and Heskett, J.L. *Corporate Culture and Performance.* New York: The Free Press, 2011).
2. Erickson, F. In D. Tannen and J.E. Alatis (eds.), *Languages and Linguistics: The Interdependence of Theory, Data and Application* (Washington, D.C.: Georgetown University Press, 1986).
3. Fisher (2000).
4. Devillard, S., Sancier-Sultan, S., Werner, C., Maller, I., and Kossoff, C. (2014). "Gender Diversity in Top Management: Moving Corporate Culture, Moving Boundaries." McKinsey & Company.
5. Mainero, L.A. (1994). "On Breaking the Glass Ceiling: The Political Seasoning of Powerful Women Executives." *Organizational Dynamics 22(4)*: 5–20.
6. Mendell, A. *How Men Think* (New York: Fawcett Columbine, 1996).
7. Tannen, D. *You Just Don't Understand: Women and Men in Conversation* (New York: Ballantine Books, 1990).

8. Ibid.

9. Kay, K., and Shipman, C. *The Confidence Code: The Science and Art of Self-Assurance—What Women Should Know* (New York: HarperCollins, 2010).

10. Epson, Laura. (2014). "Reluctant Leaders and Autonomous Followers: Leadership Tactics in Professional Services Firms." Second report for practitioners, Cass Business School.

Chapter 8

1. Goleman, D. *Working With Emotional Intelligence* (Bantam Books, 2000).

  Goleman, D., Boyatzis, R., and McKee, A. *Primal Leadership: Unleashing the Power of Emotional Intelligence* (Harvard Business Review Press, 2013).

Chapter 9

1. Mänttäri, A. (2009). "The Success Factors in Male Dominated Fields: The Case of Women in the US." Master's thesis. Jönköping International Business School.

2. Dillard, S., and Lipschitz, V. "How Female CEOs Actually Get to the Top." Harvard Business Review Website. *HBR.org*, November 6, 2014.

3. Eagly, A.H. and Carli, L.L. *Through the Labyrinth: The Truth About How Women Become Leaders* (Boston, Mass.: Harvard Business School Press, 2007).

4. Carter, N.M., and Silva, C. (2010). "Women in Management: Delusions of Progress." *Harvard Business Review.*

   Ibera, H., Carter, N.M., and Silva, C. (2010). "Why Men Still Get More Promotions Than Women." *Harvard Business Review.*

5. Mänttäri (2009).

6. Powell and Mainiero (1992).

7. Barsh, J., and Yee, L. (2012). "Unlocking the Full Potential of Women at Work." Special Report for the *Wall Street Journal.* The Executive Task Force for Women in the Economy.

8. Van Velsor and Hughes (1990).

9. Schor, S.M. "Separate and Unequal: The Nature of Women's and Men's Career Building Relationships." *Business Horizons,* September/October, 1997: 51–8.

Chapter 10

1. Linehan, M., and Scullion, H. (2008). "The Development of Female Global Managers: The Role of Mentoring and Networking." *Journal of Business Ethics 83(1)*: 29–40.

   Tharenou, P. (2005). "Does Mentor Support Increase Women's Career Advancement More Than Men's?" *Australian Journal of Management 30(1)*: 77–109.

   "Women and Mentoring: What's Working, What Isn't." Simplicity 2.0, June 19, 2014.

   "Creating Successful Mentoring Programs: A Catalyst Guide." Report. *Catalyst.org*, January 15, 2010.

   Schor (1997).

2. Fitzsimmons, T.W., Callan, V., and Paulsen, N. (2014). "Gender Disparity in the C-Suite: Do Male and Female CEOs Differ in How They Reach the Top?" *The Leadership Quarterly 25(2)*: 245–66.

3. Van Velsor and Hughes (1990).

4. Schor (1997).

5. Ibera, Carter, and Silva (2010).

6. Hansen, M.T., Iberra, H., and Peyer, U. (2010). "The Best Performing CEOs in the World." *Harvard Business Review.*

7. Ibid.

8. Henneberger, Melinda. "The Nation: Post-Monica Skittishnessl Sex, Politics and the Open Door." *New York Times*, October 10, 1999.

9. Catalyst has reported that women are "over mentored and under sponsored," indicating that this is a primary barrier to women's advancement to top leadership.

10. Schor (1997).

11. Fisher, A.B. "Dirty Little Secrets. *Savvy*, January 1998: 33–95.

12. Ibid.

13. "Can Women Succeed Without a Mentor?" *Women in the World*, April 26, 2013.

14. Fordham, S. (1988). "Racelessness as a Factor in Black Students' School Success: Pragmatic Strategy or Pyrrhic Victory?" *Harvard Business Review 58(1)*: 54–82.

   Note: This dynamic of distancing oneself from one's culture group in order to be accepted as a member in another group has been discussed in terms of African Americans taking on a "raceless-ness" in order to make white colleagues feel more comfortable with them.

Chapter 11

1. Drescher, M.A., Korsgaard, M.A., Welpe, I.M., Picot, A., and Wigand, R.T. (2014). "The Dynamics of Shared Leadership: Building Trust and Enhancing Performance." *Journal of Applied Psychology 99(5)*: 771–83.

2. Kim, W.C., and Mauborgne, R. "Blue Ocean Leadership." *Harvard Business Review*, May 2014: 60–72.

3. Venkataramani, V., Richter, A.W., and Clarke, R. (2014). "Creative Benefits From Well-Connected Leaders: Leader Social Network Ties as Facilitators of Employee Radical Creativity." *Journal of Applied Psychology 99(5)*: 966–75.

4. Ibid.

5. Hill, L.A., Brandeau, G., Truelove, E., and Lineback, K. *Collective Genius: The Art and Practice of Leading Innovation* (Boston, Mass.: Harvard Business Review Press, 2014).

6. Ibid.

7. Catmull, E. *Creativity, Inc.: Overcoming the Unseen Forces That Stand in the Way of True Inspiration* (New York: Random House, 2014).

INDEX

ABOUT THE AUTHOR

Carol Vallone Mitchell cofounded Talent Strategy Partners, a talent management consulting firm, in 2001. She has worked with numerous Fortune 500 companies and others to identify and develop leaders who will build and nurture a unique workplace culture that drives business results. She received her doctorate in Organizational Behavior from the University of Pennsylvania, where she developed a behavioral profile of success for women leaders. Continuing her research as a practitioner, she developed the Women's Leadership Blueprint™. She uses this expertise and her 20 years of leadership development experience as a go-to speaker for companies and professional associations. Her passion and success is in helping women in all fields step up to lead and succeed, and to create better organizational cultures. Carol lives in the Philadelphia area with her husband and son.

Discover YOUR collaborative leadership strengths & gaps.

The Women's Leadership Blueprint™ Assessment provides a unique look at your ability to be a strong, collaborative leader, an important area of expertise for both women and men who want to gain the respect of staff and nurture innovation. The assessment generates results that show your strengths and development gaps in each of the nine competencies discussed in this book.

You'll be surprised what you learn!

Take the Women's Leadership Blueprint™ Assessment:

Scan the QR code below or go to
https://www.learningbridge.com/TSP

TALENT STRATEGY
PARTNERS

Photo courtesy of Maura B. McConnell Photography